D0455676

Meth

America's

Drug

Epidemic

Elaine Landau

Twenty-First Century Books • Minneapolis

For Jean E. Reynolds, an outstanding editor with great taste

Twenty-First Century Books
A division of Lerner Publishing Group, Inc.
241 First Avenue North
Minneapolis, MN 55401 U.S.A.

Website address: www.lernerbooks.com

Library of Congress Cataloging-in-Publication Data

Landau, Elaine.
    Meth : America's drug epidemic / by Elaine Landau.
        p.   cm.
    Includes bibliographical references and index.
    ISBN-13: 978–0–8225–6808–7 (lib. bdg. : alk. paper)
    1. Methamphetamine—Juvenile literature. 2. Methamphetamine abuse—Juvenile literature. I. Title.
    RC568.A45L36 2008
    362.29'9—dc22   2006030923

Manufactured in the United States of America
1 2 3 4 5 6 – BP – 13 12 11 10 09 08

TABLE OF CONTENTS

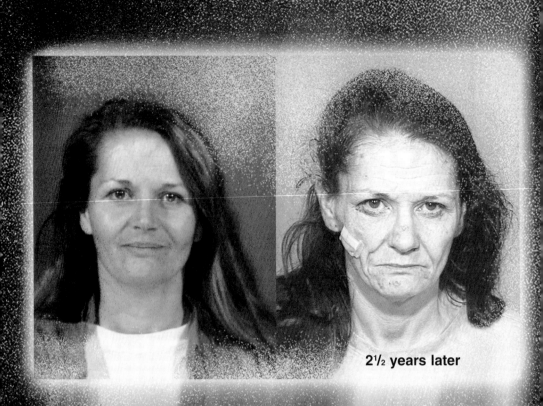

2½ years later

Chapter 1

METHAMPHETAMINE—
THE DRUG SENSATION
THAT SWEPT THE NATION

One day police arrived without warning at a middle school in a Mississippi River town. They weren't there for the school's annual Career Day or to talk to the students about street safety. Instead, they had come to arrest a sixth grader.

The boy they came for hadn't been acting like himself for months. He'd turned jittery and moody and had been having trouble sleeping. Most of the time, he seemed irritable and on edge. The smallest thing would annoy him, and he'd often fly into a rage with little provocation.

Yet his behavior wasn't the reason he caught the attention of the police. Following his arrest, the sixth grader pled guilty to a felony drug-related crime. The boy admitted that he, along with several other young people, had been organizing methamphetamine parties.

A Popular Drug In recent years, methamphetamine has become increasingly popular throughout much of the United States. The drug is a powerful and highly addictive stimulant. It produces a high that's been described as pleasurable, yet meth can ruin users' lives. Because methamphetamine is often made from lethal ingredients such as battery acid, drain cleaner, and antifreeze, its effects can be deadly.

What Is It Like? Methamphetamine is usually an odorless white to yellow powder, but it may also be brown or even green. You can buy methamphetamine in different forms. Among these are pills, capsules, powders, or chunks. It has a bitter taste, so users frequently dissolve the powder in various liquids. It can also be smoked, snorted, or injected.

Methamphetamine and Youth How does a sixth grader become involved with a potentially deadly drug? Unfortunately, there are lots of ways. In this case, the boy's first supplier was his mother's twenty-seven-year-old boyfriend. By the time the police arrived to pick up the boy, he was exhibiting visible signs of methamphetamine addiction. Luckily, there was an opening at an inpatient treatment center at the time the youth appeared in juvenile court. The judge believed that this was the right placement for him, and he was soon transferred there. His mother's boyfriend was subsequently arrested for giving drugs to a minor.

While many found it shocking to learn that a sixth grader could be organizing methamphetamine parties, the boy was certainly not the youngest methamphetamine user on record.

A Dangerous Drug by Any Name

Methamphetamine goes by many names, depending on who is using it and the part of the country where it's being used. The most common labels include meth, speed, teak, and go-fast. In its smoked form, it's frequently called ice, crystal, fire, or glass. Other names include:

Blue meth
Chicken feed
Cinnamon
Crank
Crystal meth
Geep
Granulated orange
Lemon drop
Ozs
Peanut butter
Sketch
Spoosh
Stove top
Tick tick
Trash
Wash
Ya Ba
Yellow barn
Yellow powder

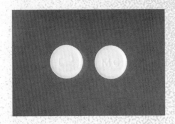

Methamphetamine not only has many names, but also many forms. *(Top to bottom)* Its original crystalline form is broken down to be sold as bags of small crystals for use in a water pipe; powder for snorting or mixing into liquid; and it is also sold in pill form.

A drug counselor in Iowa reported that she'd been treating a boy who'd used methamphetamine since he was ten. "I've seen some kids who used it and didn't even know what it was," she noted in commenting on the case.

The same drug counselor went on to say that nearly three-quarters of the teens she's treated for drug addiction have used methamphetamine. By the time they're in treatment, users are frequently more knowledgeable about what they are taking. Methamphetamine is often their drug

The availability of drugs—particularly meth—has caused raves (large dance parties featuring techno music and usually involving the taking of mind-altering drugs) to be targeted and criticized by law enforcement officials and parents' groups.

of choice because it is considered a fashionable way to get high. As the drug counselor added, "It's a trend drug right now and they want to fit in."

It's typical that the sixth grader sold this drug to others by arranging private methamphetamine parties. Methamphetamine is generally not bought or sold on city streets, like so many other illegal drugs. More often, friends or casual acquaintances supply users with this drug. According to the National Institute on Drug Abuse, "It is typically a more closed or hidden sale, prearranged by 'networking' with those producing the drug. Often it is sold 'by invitation only' at all night warehouse parties or 'raves.'"

Who Uses Methamphetamine?
The lack of street availability of this drug has not stopped its rapid spread throughout the nation. It has also become increasingly difficult to come up with a profile of the typical methamphetamine user. Cases of methamphetamine use have been cited among adults, teens, and children as well as among people of different races and income levels.

Methamphetamine's History
Methamphetamine is the more powerful cousin of the drug class known as amphetamines. Amphetamines have been around for some time—they were used in China more than five thousand years ago. Then in 1887, the German pharmacologist, L. Edleano, produced the drug chemically. However, a Japanese chemist came up with the more potent methamphetamine in 1919. During World War II (1939–1945), the governments of Germany, the United States, and Japan made it available to their soldiers. The governments believed the drug would enhance the aggression, endurance, and performance of their

WHO CHOOSES METH?

The Center for Substance Abuse Prevention cites the following groups as being especially susceptible to the illusion that using methamphetamine is beneficial:

- Truck drivers trying to remain alert during the long hours involved in cross-country hauls
- Restaurant, construction, and factory workers hoping to reduce fatigue
- People who are trying to lose weight
- White-collar workers wanting to become more competitive and able to work longer, more productive hours
- Athletes, both in and out of school, seeking temporary bursts of energy and feelings of increased physical endurance
- Youth partying all night
- Students enduring marathon study sessions
- Men in some gay populations wanting to boost sexual performance or deal with depression
- People with acquired immunodeficiency syndrome (AIDS) seeking temporary relief from AIDS-related fatigue and depression
- People manufacturing methamphetamine at home as an income source and/or to support their addiction

armed forces. Though the armed forces of all three countries used methamphetamine at times, the Japanese relied on it more extensively. Toward the end of the war, they were especially short of well-trained soldiers. They resorted to methamphetamine, hoping to keep their men awake and alert in battle and on bombing missions. The soldiers taking the drug were able to walk longer distances and run to the point of exhaustion. However, the military also had to deal with increased bouts of anxiety and panic in the men along with sleeplessness, dizziness, and heat intolerance.

Unaware of the highly addictive nature of this drug, many Japanese soldiers returned to civilian life with a serious drug habit. At first, these addicted soldiers easily found sufficient amounts of the drug to satisfy their cravings because, immediately following the war, the drug companies had plenty of stockpiled supplies to sell to the civilian population. Veterans as well as youths proved to be their best customers. The results were devastating. Within five years of the war's end, thousands of Japanese people became methamphetamine addicts. Due to extensive use of the drug, there was a considerable rise in the number of methamphetamine users experiencing heart attacks, strokes, and lung, liver, and kidney damage. Many methamphetamine users also had to deal with excessive weight loss, hallucinations, and even psychosis. The hospitals in Japan were hardly equipped to handle the related health problems that arose and the overwhelming need for treatment.

The situation grew so serious that in 1948 the Japanese parliament rushed through a law to regulate stimulants such as methamphetamine. But even this measure didn't solve the problem. The law banned methamphetamine only in powder or pill form. Liquid methamphetamine remained legal and available. The number of methamphetamine addicts continued to grow as methamphetamine users bought needles to inject the liquid form of the drug into their arms.

Realizing that they'd made a terrible mistake, the Japanese government banned all forms of methamphetamine the next year. However, ridding the population of this destructive substance was not so easy. People found it hard to quit using methamphetamine, and the drug continued to be sold in Japan illegally. By 1954 500,000 Japanese people were regularly using methamphetamine.

Methamphetamine usage also began in the United States on a broad scale in the years following the war. During the 1950s, methamphetamine was legally manufactured in the United States and sold as an over-the-counter drug known as Methedrine. Individuals needing to push their bodies to stay awake longer readily purchased the drug. As might be expected, college students staying up all night to study bought numerous packages of the drug. Truckers who needed to drive through the night to make delivery deadlines also used it. Before mandatory drug testing in athletic competitions, athletes secretly took it as well, hoping to gain an edge on their opponents.

Nevertheless, it wasn't long before negative side effects of Methedrine use began appearing. Users of Methedrine and other over-the-counter methamphetamine-based drugs suffered heart attacks and strokes—and some even died while using large doses of the stimulant. As a result, methamphetamine was removed as a component in over-the-counter pharmaceutical products.

Yet the drug remained available in the United States with a doctor's prescription. During the 1960s, it was frequently prescribed as a weight-loss drug. Taken in pill form, this medication was swallowed by fashion models in both Europe and the United States as well as by countless women who hoped to look like them. Though rarely prescribed in the twenty-first century, this drug remains legal with a legitimate prescription. At times, it is still used to treat obesity, attention deficit disorder, and several other medical conditions. Nevertheless, by the 1970s, doctors in the United

The trend toward extreme thinness that emerged in the 1960s began with fashion models, but soon made unrealistic body weight the norm. Many women and girls found that taking drugs such as amphetamines would result in rapid weight loss.

States became increasingly reluctant to prescribe this drug for their patients. The potential for abuse due to taking more than the prescribed amount was too great and the consequences too costly.

Starting in the 1970s, people who wanted methamphetamine had to buy it illegally, on the black market. At first, motorcycle gangs on the West Coast of the United States dominated this underground market. These bikers didn't just sell methamphetamine. Many were heavy users themselves. In fact, the nickname "crank" for methamphetamine came from bikers, who kept the drug in the crankcases of their motorcycles. According to the National Institute on Drug Abuse, a noticeable rise in methamphetamine use also took place at this time among the female and male prostitutes who traded sex for drugs with these motorcycle gang members.

In the 1980s, biker gangs faded into the background of the methamphetamine drug scene. Instead, Mexican drug syndicates, known as cartels, invaded the market. These suppliers were much more organized than the biker gangs had been. As Rusty Payne, a spokesperson for the federal Drug Enforcement Administration (DEA) noted, methamphetamine was becoming a major-league drug trafficked through well-run channels. "These guys are not addicts but sophisticated businessmen," Payne stated. "They're not your typical gangs who drive hot rods and beat people up. They're savvy, and they're equipped with a lot of technology." With these professional drug-trafficking organizations involved, vast quantities of the illegal substance were smuggled in from south of the border. Displaying the precision of a well-run corporation, methamphetamine labs sprang up in Mexico to produce substantial amounts of the drug in pill form. The drug cartels were soon skillfully tapped into the large consumer base of potential methamphetamine users to the north.

In the mid-1990s, the methamphetamine drug scene changed once again, and the consequences of that switch are still being felt throughout the nation. Some U.S. methamphetamine users came up with a way to manufacture their own methamphetamine. These users developed a simpler production process and posted their methamphetamine recipes on the Internet. Some users found that they were able

As part of a traveling exhibit titled, "Target America: Traffickers, Terrorists, and You," The Drug Enforcement Administration Museum shows a replica of a hotel room that has been made into an amphetamine laboratory.

to gather the chemicals and equipment necessary to easily make this drug in their own homes. Before long a growing number of methamphetamine labs popped up in houses, apartments, motel rooms, and even cars.

By cutting out the Mexican suppliers and relying heavily on inexpensive household chemicals as raw materials, these individuals manufactured methamphetamine at a fairly low cost. Not only could they meet their own need for the drug, but they could also sell the drug and make a decent profit. As makeshift methamphetamine labs came to dot the U.S. landscape, the number of methamphetamine users soared. Though the Mexican drug cartels still produced about 75 percent of the methamphetamine used in the United States, the remaining 25 percent was homemade.

Where the Drug Is
Methamphetamine first took root in rural areas of the United States. Its early production, trafficking, and abuse were centered in the western, southwestern, and midwestern states. Most methamphetamine users were poor and white, fueling methamphetamine's reputation as the favorite drug of the working poor, or the poor man's cocaine.

By the early 2000s, the drug had spread to mainstream America. By then, methamphetamine users could be found among people of all races, ages, and income levels. Housewives in Maine, teens in Pennsylvania, computer professionals in New York, and factory workers in Georgia were equally likely to become addicted. Women were just as prone to using the drug as men. For example, nearly half of the women entering a Salt Lake City, Utah, jail tested positive for methamphetamine.

The Statistics on Methamphetamine
U.S. government statistics indicate that more than 12,000,000 Americans have tried methamphetamine. Many are young people. A 1999 survey showed that 3.2 percent of eighth graders, 4.6 percent of tenth graders, and 4.7 percent of twelfth graders had used methamphetamine. As of 2006, methamphetamine labs had been identified in all fifty states.

The rapid spread of methamphetamine use created new challenges for law-enforcement agencies. In many regions, police officers have cited methamphetamine as their most difficult drug battle. In July 2005, the National Association of Counties surveyed five hundred law-enforcement agencies in

The following passage is from a former methamphetamine dealer and user, Dominic Ippollito:

"Meth was a distant second to coke [cocaine] when I began [dealing drugs] but by the end it was by far my most popular product, accounting for more than half of my sales and two-thirds of my profits. It also became my personal drug of choice and for ten years I smoked it every day. . . . Most of [my customers] were . . . hard working, productive members of society, the kind of people you'd never suspect—and rather not know—are habitual drug users. Among them, a half dozen doctors, several lawyers, two research scientists, even a police dispatcher. As my business grew, it also expanded geographically. My 'sales territory' covered most of southern California. . . . I also used overnight delivery companies to ship drugs to select points around the country: meth to New York City and San Francisco . . . . "

forty-five states regarding drug use. Fifty-eight percent of these agencies stated that methamphetamine was their greatest drug challenge. That figure contrasted sharply with the 19 percent of law-enforcement agencies listing cocaine as their greatest drug problem and the 17 percent stating that marijuana was the most problematic drug in their area.

Teens Addicted to Methamphetamine

Many young people have had frequent run-ins with the law over methamphetamine use. Young methamphetamine addicts have resorted to robbery, forgery, and fraud to get money to support their drug habit. Like many adult methamphetamine

"This stuff is so strong and so debilitating that kids who use it go downhill so quickly," noted Wayne Beatty, the safe-schools administrator for the 12,000-student Natrona County school district in Wyoming. "They drop out of school and end up in the criminal justice system."

users, they often become involved in spur-of-the-moment crimes such as purse snatchings or break-ins.

More than half of the young people doing time in the Arizona Department of Juvenile Corrections have a history of methamphetamine use. Of these, about 84 percent did methamphetamine on a regular basis, and many of these young people were high on the drug when they committed crimes. In some cases, these teens believed that being addicted to methamphetamine had cost them their humanity.

"When I do meth, it just takes over your body," noted sixteen-year-old Joseph, a recovering methamphetamine user at Adobe Mountain School in Phoenix, Arizona, (a juvenile detention facility for boys). "You don't have no feelings. You don't have no fear. You don't think."

Laura, a young recovering methamphetamine addict at a juvenile detention facility for girls, resorted to forging checks to support her methamphetamine habit. She had become pregnant at just fourteen and she'd been arrested eleven times by the time she'd turned sixteen. "When I really think about it, it hurts to think that I did all that stuff," she said. "I was heartless. I didn't care about other people."

Methamphetamine has always been dangerous, but it's been estimated that today's methamphetamine is more than six times as potent as the drugs sold by biker gangs in the 1970s. Statistics show that current methamphetamine users die from suicide, traffic accidents, and murder at rates higher than the general population. Doctors in emergency rooms where young methamphetamine addicts are frequently brought sometimes say that methamphetamine addiction can be as deadly as some types of cancer.

The personal as well as financial consequences of teens using methamphetamine were further underscored by Anthony Parrish, a licensed substance-abuse counselor and clinical specialist at the Adobe Mountain School. "It's not just the drug. It's the lifestyle," Parrish explained as he described how easily teens can slip once they've started using methamphetamine. "It's the cash and sex and drugs. It's guns and cars. The lifestyle is incredibly powerful, especially for an adolescent. I'm not surprised they do it."

Robert Pandina, a psychology professor and director of the Center of Alcohol Studies at Rutgers University in New Jersey, echoed these sentiments. "You're putting a fairly potent drug in the hands of inexperienced users," he said. "It doesn't bode well for problems on the horizon." Many educators, law-enforcement counselors, and people whose lives have been damaged by methamphetamine would agree.

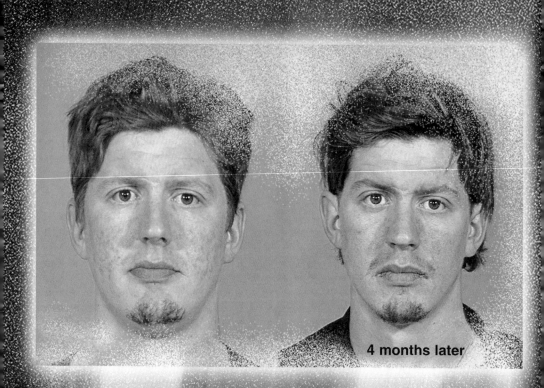

4 months later

Chapter 2

All About Methamphetamine— The Extreme Highs and Lows

Michael was a Missouri teenager who didn't think that trying methamphetamine would be very harmful. He thought of himself as a tough kid and figured that he was stronger than any drug. When he was just fifteen, he began hanging out with some friends who did methamphetamine. When they offered it to him for free, he decided to give the drug a try and began snorting it regularly.

However, Michael soon saw that he'd been wrong about this drug. Trying to stop using methamphetamine was considerably more difficult than he'd ever imagined. He didn't like needing the drug, but he couldn't help himself. It was as if he'd lost control of his life. "I got hooked right away," Michael later explained. "It took my body. It destroyed my nostrils. I couldn't blow my nose without blowing blood into the rag. It clogged up my skin and put big bumps on my face, the back of my neck."

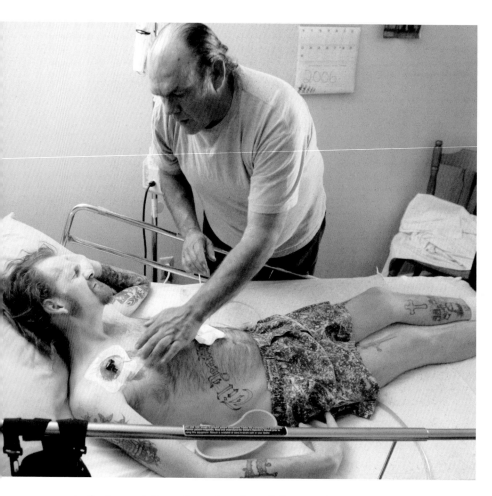

In the hope of dissuading others from following the same path, Jack Bridges allowed a documentary to be made showing how methamphetamine has ravaged the body of his thirty-four-year-old son Shawn—now confined to a hospital bed.

Like many methamphetamine users, Michael sometimes felt certain that there were imaginary bugs under his skin. He'd pick at them, causing open sores. Once he became so obsessed with biting off a hangnail that he caused his finger to bleed so badly that he needed stitches. Michael was slim when he started using methamphetamine, but he still lost a great deal of weight on the drug. He also began having seizures.

By the time he was a senior in high school, methamphetamine had played a large role in unraveling Michael's life. His world came crashing in on him that year when he was arrested on methamphetamine-related charges and sent to jail. The drug had taken its toll on both his health and his future. "I cried so hard in my bunk [in jail]," Michael later related. "I missed my family. I missed not being able to finish high school. A lot of stuff hurts you so deep down inside in ways you didn't realize. You don't have freedom when you're using this drug. The drug's got control of you."

Getting Hooked on Methamphetamine

Getting hooked on methamphetamine as Michael did is not unusual. Many teens mistakenly believe that smoking methamphetamine is not any more addictive than smoking marijuana. That isn't so. The addiction rates for methamphetamine are significantly higher than for many other drugs. In

THE TRUTH ABOUT METHAMPHETAMINE

"Sadly, people find out that meth is fun to party with," noted Dr. Susan Dreisbach, an assistant research professor at the University of Colorado in Denver. "But there are two sides—recreational and functional—and the reality is that the addiction is so powerful. For the majority of people, meth creeps up on them and becomes a daily need. Unfortunately, meth users are most likely to be discovered when they cannot meet employer expectations, when they neglect their children, or when they commit crimes. . . . "

A stint in jail or the hospital is sometimes a rude awakening for teens who are often surprised that their addiction is so out of their control.

one study, 94 percent of those who smoked methamphetamine for six months became addicted. The same was true for 72 percent who snorted methamphetamine. However, only 8 percent of people who smoked marijuana over the same time period became addicted.

Despite warnings, people often don't believe how devastating methamphetamine's effects can be. What draws people to this dangerous drug? Like Michael, many people don't think that methamphetamine can harm them. They try it, seeking a pleasurable feeling. After smoking or intravenously injecting methamphetamine, they experience an intensely pleasing feeling known as a "rush" or "flush." This sensation lasts only a few minutes but is followed by a high that may last eight to fourteen hours. When methamphetamine is snorted or swallowed in pill form, users experience the same high but not the initial intense rush.

The typical effects of a methamphetamine high include:
- Euphoria
- Alertness or wakefulness
- Feelings of increased strength and renewed energy
- Feelings of invulnerability
- Feelings of increased confidence and competence
- Intensified feelings of sexual desire

While high on methamphetamine, users feel alert, full of energy, and extremely self-confident. This occurs because after the drug enters the bloodstream, it reaches the pleasure center of the brain, causing it to release lots of a feel-good brain chemical called dopamine. The size, shape, and chemical structure of methamphetamine are very similar to dopamine. The drug produces an increase in extra energy and stamina, along with a decrease in appetite. Some people say that it feels like you're falling in love.

Crashing
In this case, though, love doesn't last very long. Soon the pleasurable feelings stop. Research shows that methamphetamine's high wears off even before the drug disappears from the user's bloodstream. The end of a methamphetamine high may be followed by an unpleasant sensation known as a crash. When crashing, or tweaking, as it is also called, methamphetamine users may feel anxious, depressed, and irritable.

Just as they previously felt filled with energy, now they may feel exhausted. Many say they feel anxious and empty at the same time. These individuals may also become paranoid and mistakenly think that the people around them are plotting against them or mean to harm them in some way.

The paranoia experienced by methamphetamine users can be disastrous. They may believe that people are trying to poison them and refuse to eat food prepared for them. They may be convinced that a faithful husband or wife or boyfriend or girlfriend has begun to cheat on them. They may threaten or spy on the innocent loved one for hours each day.

When they are in this state, some methamphetamine users may believe that people determined to control their brains have planted microphones in their homes. Many hear voices that they feel are inescapable. One methamphetamine user described what it is like: "It feels like people are reading your mind. At first, you can't quite make out what they are saying. Then the voices get too plain. I'd hear them calling my name." When crashing, methamphetamine users sometimes hallucinate. Many feel itchy and see imaginary insects crawling on or beneath their skin.

Wanting to stop the crash and feel the euphoric high again, methamphetamine users often take more of the drug. They begin bingeing or taking methamphetamine continuously for two or three days in a row without sleeping. Dr. Alex Stalcup, an addiction physician in California, some-times treats methamphetamine-addicted patients who've been up for days. Some of his methamphetamine patients have stayed awake for ten days or more. One woman he saw had been up for twenty-one days on the drug. "Politely put, she was crazier than a barn owl," Dr. Stalcup noted.

Some bingers try taking more methamphetamine every two to three hours. When methamphetamine is legitimately prescribed by a physician for a medical condition, the dose is rarely higher than 50 milligrams a day. But people using methamphetamine for recreational purposes take at least 250 milligrams to achieve the high they desire. When bingeing, it is not uncommon for someone on methamphetamine to use up to 1,000 milligrams a day.

A Brain Change Recapturing a methamphetamine high can become extremely difficult for people who've taken the drug for a long time. That's because methamphetamine causes changes in the brain. It damages the brain cells that contain the two important pleasure-related brain chemicals— dopamine and serotonin. So far, the research shows that while these brain cells don't die, their nerve endings are cut back and not much regrowth occurs. This makes it exceedingly hard for chronic methamphetamine users to experience the pleasurable feelings they once did. In fact, the National Institute on Drug Abuse warns that people who continue to use methamphetamine will eventually have a difficult time feeling pleasure from anything.

However, methamphetamine users often don't consider the potential consequences in their quest for the drug. At times their craving for the drug becomes so intense that their life revolves around getting more methamphetamine. Everything else, including school, family, friends, or work, becomes a distant second.

Scientists are conducting new research to determine how methamphetamine further changes the brain. Simply put, methamphetamine has been shown to be more toxic to the brain than many other drugs. While scientists still aren't sure, they suspect that the damage to the brain from prolonged methamphetamine use may be permanent. They've discovered that even three years after longtime methamphetamine users stopped taking the drug, the damage to their brains remained.

Not being able to undo this damage is an especially

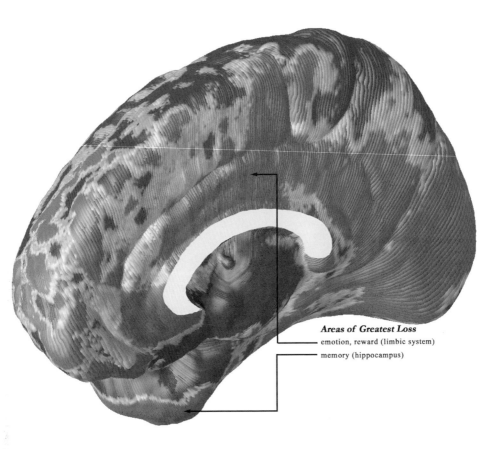

Areas of Greatest Loss
— emotion, reward (limbic system)
— memory (hippocampus)

The University of California–Los Angeles conducted the first high-resolution MRI study of individuals addicted to methamphetamine. The findings, announced in July 2004, were that the drug causes the greatest brain decay in the areas affecting emotion and memory. The darkest areas on the scan above indicate about a 5 percent tissue loss.

frightening aspect of methamphetamine use. This is not true of cocaine, another "feel-good" drug similar to methamphetamine in some ways. Cocaine is almost completely metabolized in the body and stays in the brain only a short time. However, this doesn't mean that cocaine should ever be anyone's drug of choice. Cocaine can be tremendously damaging to the body in other ways.

A 2004 study by University of California–Los Angeles (UCLA) researchers revealed that extensive methamphetamine use resulted in serious brain-cell deficits. The damage to the brain was similar to that seen in the early stages of dementia. As Dr. Daniel Amen, a clinical neuroscientist who specializes in nuclear brain imaging in northern California put it, "Our scans basically show that these people [individuals who have used methamphetamine repeatedly] are dealing with a defective brain."

WHILE TAKING METHAMPHETAMINE . . .

Below are some of the physical, emotional, and mental difficulties that people can experience when taking methamphetamine:

- Memory problems
- Insomnia
- Decreased appetite and anorexia
- Increased heart rate, blood pressure, and body temperature
- Tremors or convulsions
- Breathing problems
- Lung, kidney, and liver damage
- Irreversible damage to blood vessels in the brain, which can result in strokes
- Increased risk of getting or transmitting HIV(human immunodeficiency virus)/AIDS, hepatitis B and C, and other diseases for users who inject meth and share needles

Overdosing on methamphetamine can lead to hyperthermia (raised body temperature) and convulsions. If these conditions aren't treated promptly, the person can die.

Dr. Greg Hipskind, another California doctor, brought up still another negative effect that this drug has on the brain, adding that because methamphetamine decreases the flow of blood to the brain, "it dumbs you down."

Months after people stop using methamphetamine, they frequently report that they still feel depressed, anxious, and fatigued. Many also continue to experience paranoid feelings and exhibit aggressive behavior. Over time, reduced levels of dopamine caused by methamphetamine use can result in symptoms like those seen in Parkinson's disease. Parkinson's disease is a serious neurological disorder that causes rigidity or stiffness in the arms and legs, along with slowed movement. People with Parkinson's disease sometimes experience tremors and have balance problems.

Extreme Highs and Lows

Methamphetamine is a drug known for its extreme highs and lows. Sometimes people start taking the drug after hearing that the high they'll feel is better than anything they've ever experienced. Others may take it because they want the extra energy methamphetamine provides, or they hope to lose weight using it. They rarely think about the extreme lows that can follow the highs or the extreme side effects that often result from continually using the drug.

People who take methamphetamine for energy see themselves as being alert and efficient. Yet ongoing methamphetamine use can lead to compulsive repetitive behaviors. The U.S. government's treatment guidelines describe the following activities as typical of those that methamphetamine addicts frequently find themselves engaged in: "vacuuming the same part of the rug over and over, popping knuckles, picking at scabs, or taking apart and reassembling mechanical devices."

METHAMPHETAMINE AS A DIET DRUG— HALEY'S STORY

Haley started using methamphetamine when she was just eleven years old. Her best friend had been taking the drug, and Haley longed to be as skinny and pretty as she thought her friend was. At first, methamphetamine seemed to do the trick. Haley lost weight and her self-esteem improved.

"It [methamphetamine] makes you feel more confident about yourself and definitely more mature," Haley recalled. "I remember wearing itty-bitty tank tops and I felt like I fit into them when I was high. Girls who are overweight get into meth harder and faster than others. They think they are getting what they want."

Being thinner made Haley more comfortable around boys, and this led to her having sex with them. Then at twelve, she became pregnant and had an abortion. Feeling depressed and somewhat guilty afterward, Haley took still more methamphetamine, hoping to numb her emotional pain.

After starting high school, Haley found that her methamphetamine habit also interfered with her education. She recalled what happened: "I went to high school. [Methamphetamine] made me feel like I could do anything. I was in at least one fight every day. I would beat [up] people, but it felt good to do it when you were high."

Haley eventually quit school. She continued using methamphetamine heavily, and to support her drug habit, she started stealing merchandise from local stores. Haley went through a lot before she eventually got help, and it all began after she started using methamphetamine to lose a few pounds.

Many girls and women start on methamphetamine hoping to lose weight. They are anxious to look slim, but that description hardly describes the way chronic methamphetamine users often end up looking. A weight loss of anywhere from fifty to one hundred pounds is not unheard of for methamphetamine addicts. The consequences of such weight loss can be serious.

Dr. Karol Kumpfer, former director of the U.S. Center for Substance Abuse Prevention in Washington, D.C., had formerly worked in a northern California substance abuse treatment program. While there, she saw some young females who began taking methamphetamine to lose

The unsightly dental condition that has come to be known as "meth mouth" results from the drug's tendency to reduce the amount of saliva, the presence of which defends teeth against rotting.

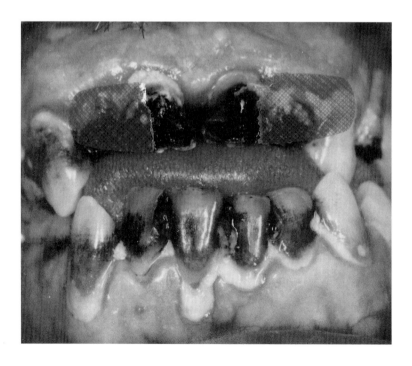

weight. These young women were not the picture of beauty they thought they'd become. Dr. Kumpfer instead described them as looking like "they had come from Auschwitz [a World War II concentration camp]."

"I was just shocked," Dr. Kumpfer noted in explaining her reaction to the exceedingly thin women. "Heroin addicts at least eat, and they hold jobs." Of course, in time, heroin takes a devastating toll on the minds and bodies of its users as well.

Besides becoming emaciated, the ongoing use of methamphetamine can cause the user's hair to fall out in clumps. Often women stop menstruating. Many lose teeth as a result of meth-related tooth decay and gum disease, a condition often known as "meth mouth." In some instances, the tooth decay resulting from methamphetamine is so severe that the teeth cannot be saved—they have to be pulled out.

Tweakers People who abuse methamphetamine regularly are known as tweakers. Tweakers can be dangerous. A person who is high on methamphetamine may not have slept in three to fifteen days and may be extremely irritable or irrationally paranoid. If that individual is using alcohol or other drugs in combination with methamphetamine, the danger can be even worse. Tweakers continually crave more methamphetamine, and this driving need has often led to unpredictable behavior and violence.

Who-Else Is Affected? The rage and paranoia methamphetamine users sometimes exhibit when they are tweaking can have terrifying consequences for those who happen to cross their paths. In areas where methamphetamine is the drug of choice, hospital emergency rooms are often filled with the victims of methamphetamine addicts.

Doctors and other hospital personnel in trauma centers have treated many methamphetamine victims who have never taken the drug. Often these individuals were beaten, stabbed, or shot by methamphetamine addicts who robbed them in a desperate attempt to get money to buy more of the drug. Friends as well as family members of sleep-deprived, irrational methamphetamine addicts who've lashed out while bingeing have made their share of appearances at hospital emergency rooms as well.

Some victims never make it to emergency rooms. In 1997 an Arizona man who was high on methamphetamine repeatedly stabbed his fourteen-year-old son. He decapitated the boy and threw his head out the window of a van. At the time, the man was convinced that the devil was inside the van with him. The man is now serving a thirty-year sentence for the crime.

Perhaps Ron Jackson, director of Evergreen Treatment Center in Seattle, Washington, best summed it up when he noted the difference between methamphetamine and heroin users. Jackson said, "People on heroin are basically going to leave you alone unless they're desperate for money. Somebody loaded on meth is going to be much more dangerous." Yet in reality, dealing with any addict in need of his or her drug can lead to trouble. It's not uncommon for heroin addicts desperate for cash to resort to violent crime.

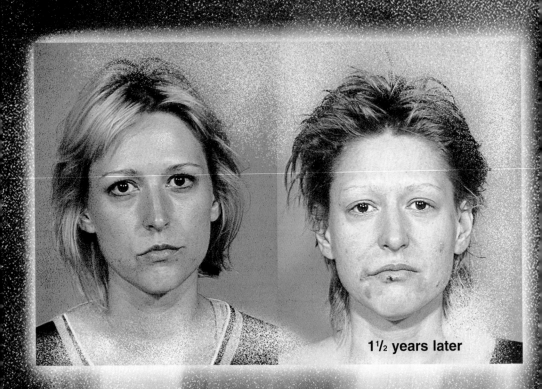

1½ years later

Chapter 3

Up Close and Personal—How Methamphetamine Affects Lives

Twenty-year-old Janelle Hornickel, the youngest of four children, had a happy childhood and a bright future. Growing up on a Nebraska farm, she'd spent her youth baking pies, being in 4-H groups, and caring for her pet chickens, cats, and a Shetland pony named Peaches.

"Janelle was a traditional girl," her mother, Twilla Hornickel, said in describing her daughter. "She always loved having the family together on the holidays—having the picnic beside the lake on the fourth of July. She always liked to have family meals, and it just wasn't a holiday without that same food she liked."

As time passed, Janelle seemed to remain very much the all-American girl. She was a cheerleader in both junior high and high school, continued with 4-H projects, and developed an interest in photography. She had a lovely singing voice and she joined the school chorus, and took part in school plays.

Janelle liked college life at Creighton University in Omaha, Nebraska, as much as she had liked high school. She so excelled at baking and sewing that she was nicknamed "Mother of the Dorm." In addition to keeping up with her studies, she found a job outside of school in the human resources department of a company she really liked.

"She didn't go back to her [hometown] friends when she left for college," Janelle's mother recalled. "She wanted to make a new life and make new friends." Yet an old friendship rekindled one year when Janelle came home from college for the summer. It was with a young man named Michael

Meth made a winter drive deadly for Janelle Hornickel *(right)* and her boyfriend, Michael Wamsley *(left)*, both just twenty years old.

Wamsley, whom Janelle had met in seventh grade.

The pair hadn't dated in junior high or high school—in fact, Michael had dropped out of high school shortly after his freshman year. But after running into each other at the local grocery store that summer, Janelle and Michael started going out and became quite close. They began living together, and Janelle hoped to help Michael get his high-school diploma and study to become a mechanic.

Their friends and family were happy for them and thought that things seemed to be looking up for this young couple—until the night of January 4, 2005. The couple was heading home to their apartment in Omaha, Nebraska, when they became caught in a major snow-storm. The first sign that they might be in trouble came at about 7:30 P.M., when they were stopped on the road by a police officer for failing to signal. At that point, the officer asked if the pair was lost. Michael and Janelle replied that they thought they were only a few blocks from their apart-ment building in Omaha.

In actuality, they were nowhere near their home. Instead, they were in Saunders County—about 120 miles (193 kilo-meters) southwest of Omaha. The police officer gave them a warning ticket and then led the young couple to the highway and pointed them in the right direction. Nevertheless, Michael and Janelle never made it home that night. About five hours later, when they were nearly 20 miles (32 km) from home, their truck spun off the road. Blizzard conditions had set in, and the couple had become completely confused as to their location.

They made their first call for help to the police just after midnight on January 5. The pair told the authorities that their truck was stuck and they were lost. More calls followed as the couple stumbled about in the darkness, trying to find their way and escape the freezing weather. A few of the calls lasted for several minutes, others were shorter. Before the couple's ordeal was over, dispatchers from Douglas, Sarpy, and Saunders counties had picked up various calls from Janelle and Michael.

Though these young people begged for help, no one was able to reach them. This was largely because the pair was unable to make their location clear to the rescuers. The couple were completely confused and appeared to be hallucinating. The situation was worsened by the fact that their calls to the police had bounced off a number of cellular phone towers, making it impossible for the authorities to pinpoint their precise location.

Little that the couple said to the police dispatchers made sense. They couldn't accurately describe their surroundings. Janelle, who reportedly sounded terrified, told the 911 operator that there were people all around her who were taking cars apart and hanging the auto parts on the surrounding trees. Michael said that they'd seen groups of Mexicans and African Americans dressed in cult outfits. He added that he didn't think they spoke English and therefore couldn't help him. Michael also said that their truck, a black 2000 Ford Ranger, had rolled over on its top and they'd been forced to leave the vehicle.

Though crews of rescuers searched for Janelle and Michael, no one could find them. The dispatchers they'd talked to were worried about the couple's safety and wondered how long they could survive in the snowstorm. Both Janelle and Michael had been shivering when they'd spoken to the police dispatchers, and the authorities feared they might freeze to death. Factoring in the wind chill, the temperature had dropped to about 10 degrees Fahrenheit (−12 degrees C) that night.

Michael Wamsley made his final call for help at about four o'clock in the morning on January 5. At that point, he was alone and gave no indication of where Janelle was. Their truck was found stuck in the snow later that afternoon. The truck had not turned over as Wamsley had described to the dispatchers. Instead, it was right-side up and still had a half tank of gas in it. The young man's cell phone as well as warm clothes for both Michael and Janelle were found inside the truck too. The truck might have proved to be the safe haven the couple needed during the snowstorm, but unfortunately, they were unable to see it as such.

Search parties were quickly organized. Everyone knew that the couple wouldn't be able to last very long in the extreme cold. The search was massive and included the use of search dogs, snowmobiles, a Nebraska State Patrol helicopter, and a skydive team. Heavy equipment was brought in to move the massive snowdrifts that had accumulated.

The next afternoon Michael Wamsley's snow-covered body was found in a nearby wooded area about 2 miles (3 km) from the truck. Search parties of public safety personnel and volunteers continued to search for Janelle. Eleven of Hornickel's sorority sisters were among those who came out to help. Each day, three to seven Hornickel family members showed up at the search site as well. At times, more than 150 people were looking for Janelle. The work was exhausting, as they had to wade through knee-deep snow in some areas. Six days later, Janelle's body was located along the banks of a frozen pond. Hornickel was wearing only a sweater, jeans, and high-heeled fashion boots. Both she and Michael had left their coats in the truck.

Everyone who knew and loved these young people wanted to know how this could have happened. It was obvious that they could have stayed in their warm clothes as the blizzard raged on. There was also enough gas left in the truck for them to have kept it running with the heat on while waiting for help. How could they have thought that the truck overturned when it hadn't? Why would they leave the truck and wander about in the storm?

Autopsies were performed on the bodies of both Michael Wamsley and Janelle Hornickel. The results of the toxicology reports were made public at a January 21, 2005, press conference at the Sarpy County Courthouse. Technically, the young couple had died of hypothermia, or exposure to the extreme cold. However, methamphetamine was found in the systems of both Janelle and Michael.

Dr. Henry Nipper, director of toxicology at Creighton University Medical Center, summed it up this way: "Both individuals were impaired at the time of their death." Dr. Nipper went on to explain that the drug was probably the cause of the hallucinations and confusion that prevented the couple from getting the help that might have saved their lives. Some people thought that the people Michael believed he saw, who didn't speak English and couldn't help them, might actually have been cattle in a pasture. "High levels of methamphetamine can result in confusion and irrational behavior," Nipper noted. "People can become very paranoid. There's a range of behaviors." The toxicologist further explained that being on methamphetamine can cause someone to feel very hot, and this may account for why the couple left their coats in the vehicle despite the freezing weather.

Janelle's and Michael's families and friends were visibly

upset over losing them. In describing her son, Wamsley's mother, Gabriele Zebert, said that if anyone were ever stranded, her son would be among those who'd offer to help. "He would put down his life for somebody else," she claimed. "He was my little hero." Fighting back her tears, Janelle's mother, Twilla Hornickel, said, "I'm glad I'm as old as I am because I won't have much time before I see her [in heaven]."

Janelle and Michael paid the ultimate price for being on methamphetamine. Their deaths were a tremendous loss, yet they were not the only young couple harmed as the result of using methamphetamine. The drug also took a terrible toll on the lives of many others. Among them were Kaitlyn and Matt, a young couple from Wisconsin.

BE AWARE OF THE RISKS!

The National Clearinghouse for Alcohol and Drug Information warns that drinking alcohol or using drugs such as methamphetamine increases your risk of injury. Higher incidences of car crashes, falls, burns, drowning, and suicide are all linked to alcohol and drug use.

Before methamphetamine came into their lives, Kaitlyn, in her early twenties, and Matt, nearly thirty, had not seemed very different from a lot of other dating couples. They liked going for walks, taking drives, and renting movies. Then one day Kaitlyn went to Matt's house and found Matt and a few friends were smoking something she'd never tried before—methamphetamine. Kaitlyn tried it that day, and the following week she smoked it again. Soon, using methamphetamine became something that she and Matt looked forward to each week.

At first, Kaitlyn had experienced some doubts about what they might be getting themselves into. She admitted that smoking methamphetamine made her "feel cool," but she worried that it might be risky. Yet Matt seemed to think it was all right, so Kaitlyn decided that it must be okay. As she put it, "he was older and I liked him, so I didn't think much about it."

After a while, Kaitlyn moved in with Matt, and methamphetamine became an increasingly important part of their lives. Before long, both of them were using it daily. They began to suffer the consequences of being on methamphetamine.

No longer the dependable employee she once was, Kaitlyn lost her job. She later went to work for her father but failed to do much better there. At that point, her methamphetamine addiction had worsened. Many days she'd go to work high and even began snorting methamphetamine in the bathroom during the day at work. She also was often late and found it hard to concentrate on her duties. Kaitlyn tried her best to cover up what was happening to her, but it didn't work. Her father fired her as well. Meanwhile, her boyfriend Matt

METHAMPHETAMINE PLUS

Among young people in high school and college, methamphetamine is frequently used in combination with other drugs. Young people entering drug-treatment centers sometimes listed cocaine, marijuana, and alcohol as drugs they were using while taking methamphetamine. However, alcohol was the drug cited most often.

was on a downward spiral too. Not only was he using methamphetamine regularly, but he had also begun to drink heavily.

Kaitlyn and Matt had a friend who was a drug dealer. He introduced the pair to a purer, stronger form of methamphetamine that he referred to as "glass." "The high was just euphoric," Kaitlyn said in describing what smoking the more potent form of methamphetamine was like. "You felt invulnerable. You didn't think about any bad things."

Yet bad things began happening to the couple frequently. Unable to hold down jobs or pay their bills, their day-to-day world was collapsing. The drug also made it hard for the two to have a normal relationship. Kaitlyn found that she was no longer able to be as close to Matt as she had once been.

"He'd see shadows and get paranoid," Kaitlyn said. "He'd hear a noise and think there were people in the attic. He became really possessive. He'd get angry and accuse me of being with other guys. He wouldn't want me out of his sight."

Kaitlyn wasn't doing very well either. She dropped down to 90 pounds (41 kilograms) and was at that weight when she learned she was pregnant. Paranoid and delusional, Matt was hardly overjoyed with the news. Instead, he claimed that the child wasn't his and felt more certain than ever that Kaitlyn had been with other men. Despite her condition, Matt would sometimes push Kaitlyn around and once even slapped her.

Finding it too hard to quit the drug, Kaitlyn kept smoking methamphetamine throughout her pregnancy. She even used the drug the day before she gave birth. Then after she went into labor, she delayed going to the hospital because she feared the staff there would know that she'd been using drugs.

She was right—methamphetamine was detected in her baby's system. The child welfare authorities were alerted, and Kaitlyn almost lost her child before she had a chance to bring the baby home from the hospital. Kaitlyn was given another chance, however. She was allowed to keep the child as long as she stayed off drugs.

Kaitlyn tried her best to give up methamphetamine, and at first things looked promising. Believing that she could be a good mother, she started taking proper care of both the child and herself. Perhaps she became overconfident, though, because after a while she began to believe that she could start using methamphetamine again and stop whenever she wished. She couldn't, and it wasn't long before the authorities

METHAMPHETAMINE AND PREGNANCY DON'T MIX!

According to the Center for Substance Abuse Prevention, using methamphetamine or other drugs during pregnancy can be extremely harmful to newborns. Often these babies are born premature, or earlier than they should be. This puts them at risk for a number of difficulties.

One of the most serious is bleeding in the brain. A severe brain bleed can sometimes result in brain damage. Another serious complication that many premature infants face is respiratory distress syndrome, or RDS. Babies with RDS lack a substance that keeps the small air sacs in their lungs from collapsing. Babies exposed to drugs while in their mother's womb also often exhibit abnormal reflexes and extreme irritability. In many cases, learning disabilities become apparent once the child starts school.

found out and Kaitlyn's baby was placed in foster care.

Kaitlyn was distraught over the loss of her child and desperately wanted the baby back. That proved to be the incentive she needed to go into treatment and finally kick her methamphetamine habit. She brought pictures of her baby along with one of his blankets with her to the rehabilitation center to remind her of what was at stake as she struggled to get off methamphetamine for good. "I was going through withdrawal from my baby," she said. "I was determined that I was going to do anything—absolutely anything—that I had to do to get him back."

Kaitlyn was able to get off methamphetamine and stay off drugs. She got a job and went back to school. Matt kicked his habit, too, and the couple's child was eventually returned to them. Though staying off methamphetamine has not always been easy for Kaitlyn, she knows that she could lose her child again if she slips, and she is not willing to risk that.

Meth–Affecting People in All Walks of Life

The devastating effects of methamphetamine have not just been limited to young people. Methamphetamine victims have included successful executives in various businesses in many parts of the country. Among these was a thirty-one-year-old computer systems manager who worked for a global pharmaceutical corporation in Southern California. Besides supervising a staff of more than thirty-five people, this enterprising executive had to answer to numerous division heads. While the typical workweek is about forty hours, his workweeks were often forty-eight hours or longer.

Though this computer systems manager was both highly effective and highly paid, for years he felt as if he were working in a pressure cooker. Now and then he had turned to methamphetamine for an energy boost and a way to relieve his tension. He believed that the drug fit his lifestyle perfectly. As he often had to work late, methamphetamine helped keep him awake and alert. He described the feeling this way: "It felt like having fifteen cups of cappuccino all at once."

This successful executive had first tried the drug when he was in college and his roommate had given him some. "One of my roommates was telling me how this stuff was great," he recalled. "You could literally take it and be wired for a while and it wouldn't affect you that much and you'd be super-productive."

He began taking the drug every few weeks as an aid to help him study. Yet he found that he enjoyed the pleasurable aspects of using methamphetamine as well. "Everything—be it sex, the ability to concentrate, my sense of smell—was heightened," he said. "And I loved to eat when I was high. I'd make a hamburger, and it was the most incredible thing I'd ever eaten."

Unfortunately, the young man's dependence on methamphetamine didn't end with his college graduation. Whenever things became especially pressured at work, he'd turn to methamphetamine, regarding it as his own personal source of energy and power. In some ways, methamphetamine made him feel like a superhero. On it, he felt confident and able to accomplish a full day's work in a matter of hours.

However, it wasn't long before he began relying on the drug more often, and the negative aspects of regularly using methamphetamine surfaced. In time, it became apparent that the computer systems manager wasn't controlling his use of the drug any longer. The drug was beginning to control him.

TRUTH IS STRANGER THAN FICTION

Difficulties with coworkers are a common consequence of methamphetamine use. Yet in rare instances, use of the drug has been tolerated and even unofficially encouraged by employers hoping to speed up their staff to meet pressing deadlines. Such behavior is both illegal and unethical.

Often in such instances, the supervisor and staff member got along well beforehand. Dr. Hans Geisse, an addiction specialist at a clinic in Moreno Valley, California, noted that at times the supervisor will simply suggest something like, "Gee, if we do this [use methamphetamine], we'll be able to finish this project." One woman, who'd already been using methamphetamine, said that at one point her boss had actually given her the drug. He'd said, "Here's a bag of overtime."

He was often irritable and found it hard to be patient, even though dealing well with others was crucial to his success. Aware that his behavior was not acceptable, he tried hard to control his emotions and actions while on methamphetamine, but this was nearly impossible to do.

Eventually, all the gains that this once successful computer systems manager had worked so hard to achieve began to fall apart. As might be expected, using the drug hurt his marriage and family life. And eventually his erratic behavior hurt him at work. Undoubtedly, he would have gone much further professionally, if he hadn't relied on methamphetamine to begin with.

The computer systems manager's story is hardly an oddity when it comes to the ultimate impact methamphetamine can have on people anxious to get ahead. Unfortunately, many individuals in both school situations and the workplace mistakenly believe that they are increasing their productivity by using methamphetamine. Very often these people come to feel that they can't get through the day without their meth fix. They'll bring the drug to work or school with them and use it anywhere on the premises where they think they won't be discovered.

Therefore, methamphetamine users sometimes end up taking their drug in restrooms, a stairwell, or a private office. At times, people have even left work or school to do meth in their cars. One common clue that this might be happening occurs when a person goes into a bathroom stall and leaves without flushing the toilet. Then minutes later, that individual appears back in the classroom or work area, possibly sniffling or playing with his or her nose.

It isn't usually hard to spot a full-blown methamphetamine user in work or school situations. They are the on-edge, fidgety, and often aggressive individuals who talk too much and too quickly. However, before methamphetamine users get to that stage, they can be hard to spot. Known as maintenance users, some people manage to use small amounts of the drug over a period of time before turning into heavy users or addicts.

Initially, these individuals seem to possess the traits that employers respond to positively—they never seem to run out of energy and are able to put in long hours. As Carol Falkowski, a drug researcher at the Hazelden Foundation put it, "There are definitely people who can hide [their drug use]." Nevertheless, in most cases, their need for this highly addictive drug intensifies, and as this happens their hopes, dreams, and lives eventually shatter. The faces of methamphetamine abusers—up close and personal—are painful to see.

How Can You Tell If a Friend Is on Methamphetamine?

The Center for Substance Abuse Prevention warns that it's not always easy to tell if a friend is using methamphetamine, especially at first. Nevertheless, there are signs that you can look for. Symptoms of methamphetamine use may include the following:

- Inability to sleep
- Increased sensitivity to noise
- Nervous physical activity, like scratching
- Irritability, dizziness, or confusion
- Extreme anorexia (loss of appetite and weight loss)
- Tremors or even convulsions
- Increased heart rate and blood pressure
- Presence of inhaling paraphernalia, such as razor blades, mirrors, or straws
- Presence of injecting paraphernalia, such as syringes, heated spoons, or surgical tubing

4 years later

Chapter 4

THE METHAMPHETAMINE LAB— THE DANGER JUST NEXT DOOR

It was a cool autumn evening in rural Scottsville, Kentucky, when twenty-seven-year-old Ricky and his friend decided to get together. The young men weren't going bowling or to see a movie that night. Instead, they'd decided to cook up a batch of methamphetamine in their crude trailer lab.

The friends, who both used methamphetamine, had done this often, and by now they'd become somewhat experienced at producing their drug of choice. Yet this time things didn't go quite as expected. As Ricky watched the mixture brewing, he thought that it might be getting too hot too soon and tried to adjust their homemade equipment. That's when the trouble started. The highly combustible concoction spilled out onto the burner and burst into flames. Unfortunately, Ricky didn't have time to get out before the explosion.

"I felt my face just melting," he later said in describing the incident. "The skin was running down my arm . . . like lard." The twenty-seven-year-old could have died, but he did not. Instead, he received emergency care and was eventually treated for severe burns at the Vanderbilt University Burn Center in North Nashville, Tennessee. As it turned out, he had to endure a long and painful recovery—nearly half of his body had been badly burned.

It's a horrific story, yet what happened to Ricky is not unusual in the world of methamphetamine manufacturing. Selena was just nineteen when she was admitted to the Vanderbilt University Burn Center. Like Ricky, she'd been cooking methamphetamine when the concoction exploded. There had been many close calls before it happened. Selena explained that she and her friends "were always on pins and needles" whenever they'd accidentally spill chemicals or start small chemical fires at their makeshift methamphetamine lab.

Nevertheless, they somehow managed to keep things under control until the day of the explosion. After that, it was up to the Vanderbilt doctors to try to put things right for Selena. The task they faced wasn't easy. The doctors actually had to scrape melted plastic from the methamphetamine lab's walls off the girl's face.

As the number of methamphetamine labs has increased, so has the danger. As many as one-third of the patients at Vanderbilt University Burn Center, where Ricky and Selena were treated, have been in methamphetamine-making accidents, and it's the same story at numerous burn centers throughout the country. It's been estimated that 1 out of every 7 patients admitted to University Hospital, Denver's premier burn center, is there as a result of a methamphetamine lab explosion. "There's a break in reality between wanting to make the drugs and realizing what tremendous risk you are placing yourself in," noted Paul Bauling, director of the hospital's burn unit. "You're going to damage and cook your brain when you use [meth] but you're going to damage and cook your skin when you make it."

The physician's work is further complicated by the fact that many of these burn victims lie about their injuries, hoping to conceal their illegal involvement in drug-making operations. As Dr. Bauling further noted, "Most people don't walk in the door and say, 'Oops, I got burned in a meth lab.'" Usually they'll make up an excuse and say something like the water heater blew up.

But often there are telltale signs as to what really occurred. Frequently, these burn victims are driven up to the door of the emergency room in a car that quickly speeds away. Sometimes it may be hours before they are brought in for help, to give their associates time to clean up the lab and get away. Some patients actually go blind because they've refused to tell the doctors precisely how they were burned. This happens when certain chemicals seep into the patient's eyes and melt their corneas. It takes a few days for this to occur, and once it's happened, the damage cannot be reversed.

Though doctors have been forced to become used to treating the victims of methamphetamine-lab explosions, their work is never easy. These patients frequently suffer deeper chemical burns than the average burn victim does. It also often takes longer to resuscitate them. And because of the severity of the damage to their lungs, victims of methamphetamine lab explosions frequently spend more time on ventilators than other burn victims do.

Sometimes patients remain in the hospital for months.

Many undergo painful treatments attempting to regain the full use of their limbs. Often, extensive skin grafts are necessary as well. Burn-center physicians repeatedly warn their patients not to go back to using and manufacturing methamphetamine. They'll tell them, "This is going to kill you. If it doesn't kill you, it's going to ruin the rest of your life. . . . You may never be able to use your hands again. You may never be able to put a hamburger in your mouth. The high isn't worth the risk."

However, doctors as well as other personnel at burn units have seen that it often isn't long before their patients again put their lives in jeopardy. Many go back to using as well as making methamphetamine. Ricky, who'd been treated at Vanderbilt, began snorting methamphetamine again less than a month after he was discharged from the hospital. "I felt bad, like I let everybody down," he explained. Yet he quickly added that for him, methamphetamine was "Lucifer [the devil] himself." When it came to this drug, he felt out of control and unable to stay away from it.

Here, There, and Everywhere Methamphetamine labs have been found in all fifty states. Between 2002 and 2004, Missouri authorities uncovered more than 8,000 methamphetamine labs in that state alone. Nationally, law-enforcement officials uncover an average of 45 methamphetamine labs or dump sites each day.

At times, the most unlikely people can turn into methamphetamine makers. These would include Kimberly, an upper-middle-class woman who'd moved into an expensive home with her husband in an upscale suburb of Chicago, Illinois. Before long the couple had two sons and a dog, and to the outside world, they seemed to be living the American dream.

INDIAN COUNTRY AFFECTED BY METHAMPHETAMINE

Unfortunately, the use of methamphetamine has skyrocketed on Native American reservations in recent years. Statistics reveal that Native American communities (American Indians, Alaska Natives, and Native Hawaiians) experience the highest levels of methamphetamine use of any ethnic group nationwide. According to a Navajo Nation police officer interviewed in 2005, methamphetamine-related arrests had grown by 100 percent in the last five years. Jackie Johnson, the executive director of the National Congress of American Indians, feels that methamphetamine dealers have targeted Native American groups nationwide because reservation police forces are often small and because most reservations are remote.

To try to change the situation, a new public awareness campaign targeting methamphetamine abuse on reservations has been launched. The ground-breaking effort carries a $300,000 budget and is sponsored by a coalition of groups that includes the National Congress of American Indians, the Partnership for a Drug-Free America, the U.S. Department of Health and Human Services, the Office of National Drug Control Policy, and the U.S. Department of the Interior.

In commenting on the initiative, Jackie Johnson noted, "This new partnership will save lives . . . we can educate Indian Country on the deadly effects of methamphetamine use and begin turning the tide on its grip on our people. While Indian Country may have been hit the hardest by meth, we have to seize the opportunity to create innovative solutions."

These feelings were echoed by Carole Lankford, vice-chairwoman of the Confederated Salish and Kootenai Tribes, who is all too familiar with the devastation methamphetamine can cause in a community. Over the last four years, Tribal Social Services of the Confederated Salish and Kootenai Tribes has placed more than thirty-five meth-affected children in the tribal foster care system.

Yet a closer look at their lives revealed something far less desirable. Kimberly had become hooked on methamphetamine. Even after going to a rehabilitation facility, she had been unable to stop using the drug. Strung out and high most of the time, she could not properly care for her children. Her seemingly incurable addiction took a serious toll on her marriage as well. Before long her husband moved out and started divorce proceedings.

Despite the consequences, Kimberly was still unable to give up methamphetamine, and her life continued to spin out of control. As her drug habit worsened, so did her prospects for a better future. She became involved in making methamphetamine as well as using it.

Things really worsened for Kimberly following her three arrests for shoplifting. The last arrest had been for stealing an over-the-counter cold medication, which contained a component commonly used to make methamphetamine. It wasn't long before the authorities became aware of the methamphetamine making operation.

By the time the police arrived at her house with a search warrant, Kimberly looked nothing like she had just a few years earlier. She'd lost 45 pounds (20 kg), and her leg was badly scarred due to a severe chemical burn. The police found another ingredient used to make methamphetamine in a propane tank on her property. Kimberly was arrested that day and led away in handcuffs.

Yet the police still had more to do because the existence of Kimberly's meth lab also potentially had serious consequences for her neighbors. Close to one hundred homes in the vicinity had to be evacuated in case the meth lab exploded before it could be completely dismantled and cleaned up.

Because the chemicals used to make meth are so flammable, small household meth labs are often discovered when they ignite. Here Drug Enforcement Administration officers examine items used to make methamphetamine that were found in a house by firefighters in Saint Louis, Missouri.

Methamphetamine labs are dangerous places, and far too many of them are actively operating throughout the country today. These labs are typically small, with the average meth lab operator producing about four to six batches of methamphetamine a month. That is usually enough for the operator and a few close friends. The operator sells what's left over to get money to buy the chemicals for the next batch.

Sites that produce methamphetamine are called labs, but they are actually nothing like a legitimate pharmacological laboratory. This may be partly because illegal methamphetamine labs can be set up almost anywhere. They've been found in apartment houses, garages, sheds, barns, motel rooms, vacant buildings, and even car trunks.

Methamphetamine labs have also been uncovered out-doors, at such unlikely places as campgrounds and rest areas alongside highways. Some methamphetamine makers continually change their lab sites. Since methamphetamine can be produced in as short a time as six to eight hours, the cookware and apparatus is often dismantled and moved to another location to avoid detection.

Easy Access to Ingredients The equipment

needed to start a methamphetamine lab is readily available, as are the ingredients necessary to whip up a batch of the drug. The most common ingredients used to make methamphetamine are a variety of everyday over-the-counter drugs. Highly flammable household products may be used in the mix as well. The manufacturing process frequently calls for corrosive products from drain cleaners and an acid used in pools and spas. All these items can be purchased at pharmacies or various supply stores. They are reasonably priced and may be bought in large quantities. Illegal methamphetamine labs can be set up in almost no time. Too often people have done this, not realizing that they are dealing with a highly explosive combination of chemicals which could easily explode at any time.

Beware of Danger Often the people running

methamphetamine labs are using high levels of the drug themselves. While cooking the methamphetamine, they may feel irritable, agitated, or paranoid. Being in a highly unstable state while working with the explosive and toxic chemicals used to make methamphetamine can spell trouble.

To worsen matters, safety equipment rarely exists in illegal methamphetamine labs. Careless handling as well as overheating highly volatile chemicals or waste products has resulted in explosions and fires. Just a cigarette spark can ignite highly combustible materials left out indiscriminately. Though there are different methods of making methamphetamine, most involve the "meth cook"—handling highly flammable chemicals in the presence of an open flame or heat source. Therefore, the risk of an explosion or fire is always high.

Yet even without an explosion, methamphetamine labs make people sick. These places aren't just problems for the

A LOOK AT A METHAMPHETAMINE LAB

A makeshift meth making operation may look like a chemistry lab gone wrong. A Drug Enforcement Administration agent who'd spent years trying to close down meth labs described his first look at one this way:

I still remember walking into the farmhouse where manufacturers were cooking the drug. The chemicals looked like flour and rock salt. And then there was all that intricate glassware and tubing: If it hadn't been for the surrounding trash and filth—and the whole place hadn't smelled like a roomful of urine-soaked diapers on a hot summer day—it would have been a scene out of a college biology class. Back then, when we raided meth labs, we would just hold our breath. None of us knew to wear protective gear to guard against the chemicals that could have easily seared our lungs or blinded us for life. We just didn't know the extent of the dangers in those early days.

meth makers. At times, police officers, firefighters, para-medics, and other first responders have suffered what is known as acute exposure (to harmful chemicals), or exposure that occurs over a relatively short period of time, which can still result in health problems. This has sometimes occurred during or just after a methamphetamine operation has been raided.

Being exposed to high levels of the contaminants in meth labs can cause shortness of breath; dizziness; lack of coordination; eye and tissue irritation; chemical burns to the skin, eyes, mouth, and nose; and even death in some cases. Those arriving on the scene before the lab has been ventilated may suffer these reactions. Less severe symptoms can also occur following the raid but before the lab has been thoroughly cleaned. These symptoms frequently include headache, nausea, dizziness, and fatigue and lethargy.

The manufacture of methamphetamine has presented serious challenges for police and firefighters who may be needed in emergencies but don't always know if they are entering a highly toxic environment. This once happened when onlookers called for an ambulance to come to the scene of a traffic disturbance in the middle of an extremely busy four-lane highway. Witnesses reported that a car had stopped on the road after its interior filled with a cloudy vaporous substance. The driver and three passengers had fled the vehicle and now seemed disoriented and were coughing violently.

When an ambulance crew arrived at the scene to help, the noxious fumes overwhelmed the paramedics as well. As it turned out, the people in the car had just stolen a container of chemical gas for their meth lab. The chemical gas had accidentally been released in the vehicle. This particular chemical gas has a pungent, suffocating odor

The Effects of Long-Term Exposure to Meth-Lab Chemicals

As of yet, there isn't a lot of research on the effects of being exposed to meth lab chemicals for a long period such as months or years. Yet there have been some human and animal studies measuring the toxicity of some of the individual chemicals used to make methamphetamine. The range of health problems that can result from being exposed to these for an extended time includes cancer; liver, kidney, and brain damage; birth defects; and miscarriages.

and contact with its vapors can damage eyes and mucous membranes. Situations like these pose serious challenges for emergency workers.

Therefore, people who suspect that there's a methamphetamine lab in their area should never investigate the situation on their own. In these cases it's best to immediately notify the authorities. Being in a methamphetamine lab during an explosion can result in serious injury or death. Even touching contaminated glassware or needles can cause skin burns or poisoning. Handling items in a methamphetamine lab can also be extremely dangerous because some of the chemicals may explode on contact with air or water.

At times, methamphetamine cooks have abandoned their labs when they suspect that the police are closing in on them. In these cases, they may not have had time to dismantle their apparatus and take it with them. The potentially explosive and very toxic chemicals left behind pose a serious threat to those living nearby.

In other cases, the chemicals used to make methamphetamine have been burned or dumped in nearby wooded areas or vacant lots or alongside roads. This can be hazardous to those who live, eat, or walk near these sites. The average methamphetamine lab produces 5 to 7 pounds (2 to 3 kg) of toxic waste for every pound of methamphetamine manufactured. When the waste is disposed of improperly, it can contaminate the soil and water supplies nearby.

IS THERE A METHAMPHETAMINE LAB NEAR YOU?

The following signs indicate that a methamphetamine lab might be in operation:

- There are strong chemical odors in the air—it may smell like cat urine, ammonia, or nail polish remover.
- Lights are left on for long periods.
- Residences have windows blacked out.
- Kitchen and bathroom fixtures are chemical stained.
- Renters pay their landlords only in cash.
- There is activity at all hours of the day and night.
- There is excessive trash, containing a large number of packages of over-the-counter cold pills and chemical containers.
- Porch lights are left on at certain predetermined times as a code to indicate that drugs are available.
- Drug paraphernalia litter is scattered in the area.
- Occupants appear unwelcoming and are extremely secretive about their activities.
- Large numbers of cigarette butts are strewn outside the residence (smoking inside a methamphetamine lab can cause an explosion).

Endangered Children

Although anyone can be harmed by exposure to a methamphetamine lab's chemicals, infants and children are in the greatest danger. Sadly, every year, police reports indicate that thousands of children are found living in homes that double as methamphetamine labs. Children have higher metabolic and respiratory rates than adults, and their central nervous systems are still developing. This leaves their bodies more vulnerable to the effects of toxic chemicals.

In addition, because of their age, children are more likely to be in the path of the greatest exposure. According to the U.S. Department of Justice's Office for Victims of Crime, children living in methamphetamine labs frequently swallow or inhale toxic substances used in making methamphetamine. They are also likely to receive accidental skin pricks from discarded needles or other drug paraphernalia. Some young people residing in methamphetamine labs come in contact daily with toxic substances left on their toys, clothing, or food.

Methamphetamine labs are often filthy and frequently have no heat in the winter or air-conditioning in the summer. It's not unusual to walk into one of these home meth labs and see dirty clothes and garbage piled high on the floor. During raids, federal drug enforcement agents have sometimes opened refrigerators to find toxic chemicals next to baby-food jars. Meth labs are also often infested with a broad array of bugs and insects. Cockroaches, fleas, ticks, and lice regularly inhabit these places. Child protective services workers have also frequently found that children living in these environments are more likely to suffer from bug bites and infections as well as from burns, bruises, and untreated skin disorders.

The vicious dogs sometimes brought in to protect the premises further endanger children who live in homes that function as methamphetamine labs. At times, these dogs have turned on very young children and attacked them. The animals' feces also add to the unsanitary conditions where small children eat, play, and sleep.

Children growing up in meth labs are frequently harmed in other ways as well. People who use and manufacture methamphetamine tend to be far from ideal parents. Individuals high on methamphetamine are usually irritable and easily excitable. They can have episodes of violent behavior, confusion, and anxiety. These individuals tend to lack the patience and judgment to properly care for a child.

THE LIFE OF A TWO-YEAR-OLD IN A METH-LAB HOME

During a raid on a home-based methamphetamine lab in California, police found a two-year-old girl sitting alone in a corner. Both of the little girl's parents had used and manufactured methamphetamine. The child wasn't well. She had seeping open sores around her eyes, and on her forehead what looked like a bad burn. Once she was taken to a doctor, her condition was diagnosed as repeated, un-treated insect bites.

One man involved in manufacturing methamphetamine used his young son to try to avoid arrest. He hid a jar of highly volatile liquid methamphetamine beneath his child's car seat while his son was in the seat. In another case, a young married couple was arrested for operating a methamphetamine lab. The pair was so high on the drug at the time that they didn't even ask where their two children—an infant and a toddler—were. Fortunately, the children were safe with child protective services workers.

Brittany, a young mother and former methamphetamine addict, described what it was like to have a child with her at a methamphetamine lab:

I began hanging out with people that "cooked" meth. It was the scariest thing in my life. I was a monster on meth. I didn't care about anything but getting high. So many people take it lightly. But when you are in a room with people that you know have been up for a week, and you are helping them mix chemicals you know can explode and you are touching them, and mixing them, and heating things up that actually start fires, and yet you don't care, that is freaky. To think that I really didn't care at the time. I was always nervous when I was doing that, to the point of it making me sick to my stomach, but yet I still did it. I could have been killed or in fact killed my son in the process. I thought about those things but not too in depth or I wouldn't have been doing it. It is just a scary feeling to think, "Oh this stuff might blow up in a minute and me and my child will be dead or in the hospital." Or to think, "If the cops come right now, I would never see my son again, and I will go to jail."

Often parents operating meth labs are so consumed by the drug that they lack the capacity to see to even the child's most basic needs. This results in children from meth-lab homes not getting the medical or dental care they need. Proper nutrition, hygiene, and grooming are also usually not available to such youngsters. Sometimes after a methamphetamine binge, an addicted parent will sleep for days. In these cases, children in meth labs are left on their own. That was the case with a four-year-old boy from Colorado named Romeo. U.S. attorney general Alberto Gonzales told Romeo's story at the National District Attorneys Association meeting in Portland, Maine, in 2005. He noted:

> Romeo's parents were running a methamphetamine lab in their home. One day, at five o'clock in the morning, a SWAT team was making the final preparations to execute a search warrant on the lab. As the final checks were made, one of the detectives on surveillance reported that he saw a "skeleton" coming out the front door.
>
> His fellow officers thought he must have been hallucinating. But then his colleagues got a better look and saw the same thing: It was Romeo dressed in a skeleton costume and looking up and down his street. The officers first thought he was acting as a lookout for his parents.
>
> An officer later approached Romeo. He asked Romeo why he was dressed in a skeleton outfit and standing on his front porch. And why he was looking up and down the street at such an early hour in the morning.
>
> Romeo's eyes lit up as he explained that later that day his nursery school was holding a Halloween party. As he told the story, his shoulders slumped. He told the officer that he really wanted to go to the party but he hadn't been able to wake up his mom for the last few days and didn't know where the bus stop was. Romeo said that he thought that if he got up early enough and put his costume on, he might be able to see the bus and catch it as it drove by.
>
> At four years old, Romeo could not count to ten. But as officers later learned, he could draw a picture—in detail—of an entire meth lab operation.

> Sadly . . . Romeo's story is all too familiar: It is the story
> of the scourge of methamphetamine.

Gonzales went on to relate another incident that involved a meth lab and children in a Missouri home. He described the scene as follows:

> Three children under the age of five were living in abysmal surroundings. The rugs and counters were soaked with the toxic chemicals associated with meth production. The home was infested with roaches and rodents. There was no electricity or running water for the children. In the midst of this squalor, the meth cooks kept their prize possessions: two well-fed, well-groomed guard dogs who ate off dinner plates.
>
> And as this story and the story of Romeo show, meth's collateral damage spreads far beyond the drug manufacturer and even the end meth user. Meth is a drug that crushes the dreams and the potential of thousands of children who grow up around this dangerous drug.
>
> From 2000 to present, more than 15,000 children have been affected by methamphetamine labs and related incidents. The burn center at Arkansas Children's Hospital reports that at any time 30 to 90 percent of its patients are being treated for injuries from meth lab explosions.

The U.S. Department of Justice described additional dangers faced on a daily basis by children growing up in meth-lab homes:

> Explosives and booby traps (including trip wires, hidden sticks with nails or spikes, and light switches or electrical

appliances wired to explosive devices) have been found at some meth lab sites. Loaded guns and other weapons are usually present and often found in easy-to-reach locations. Code violations and substandard housing structures also endanger children. They may be shocked or electrocuted by exposed wires or as a result of unsafe electrical equipment or practices. Poor ventilation, sometimes the result of windows sealed or covered with aluminum foil to prevent telltale odors from escaping, increases the possibility of combustion and the dangers of inhaling toxic fumes.

One of the most tragic social effects of the meth epidemic is the fate of the many children whose parents have become involved in production of the drug.

Age and Exposure to Meth-Lab Chemicals

The potential health risks of being exposed to the chemicals used in creating methamphetamine depend on the following factors:

- The age and health of the person being exposed—children are considered among the most vulnerable.
- The specific chemicals to which the individual is exposed.
- How much of each chemical the person is exposed to.
- How long the person is exposed to the chemicals.

When their parents are unavailable for one reason or another, children living in methamphetamine labs are even less safe than usual. Relatives or other adults who are either living in the home or there to buy drugs have sometimes abused young children. Depending on the situation, the abuse may be emotional, physical, or sexual. Conflicts frequently break out in meth labs as well. It's not uncommon for children living in meth-lab homes to have seen beatings, stabbings, or police raids in which their parents were taken off to jail. Seeing their parents or caregivers as helpless in a crisis only underscores the young person's own feelings of helplessness.

Children removed from home meth labs by the authorities lose everything that is familiar to them. They are not permitted to take even items such as blankets or stuffed animals they are attached to. All items at a methamphetamine-lab site are considered contaminated. Washing a child's personal items is not even an option, since contaminated water should not be released into a septic system or city sewer.

It's unrealistic to think that children growing up in a home that's a meth lab will not be affected emotionally and socially by their surroundings. Children growing up this way may have been neglected for so long that they sometimes shut down emotionally. Some are unable to develop the normal attachments to those around them that other children do.

The trauma and stress these young people have experienced often leave them with low self-esteem, feelings of shame, and poor social skills. They tend to do poorly in school situations. Often, they feel isolated from the other students and have a hard time making friends. They also tend to have higher absenteeism rates and lower test scores than their classmates.

Teens living in these situations frequently become involved in delinquent acts and teen pregnancy. If they don't get the help they need, many go on to follow in their parents' footsteps. Young people need to be taken out of homes that serve as methamphetamine labs. If they aren't, the cost in human suffering is great.

The Washington State Methamphetamine Initiative put together the following fictional portrait of a young girl living in a home that's a methamphetamine lab. Though this girl isn't real, there are thousands of children living her life in the United States today. It's a situation that calls out for change.

Angie's Story

In the morning, Angie wakes up to go to get ready for school. There are no lights this morning because there is no electricity. And to warm the house from the cold, heat came from the gas stove with its door open last night.

It wasn't a very restful night. Angie had trouble sleeping—again—because of the noise and all the people coming and going—all night long. And it's hard to get comfortable sleeping on the floor.

Although she's tired, she pulls herself together because she hopes to have breakfast at school. There is no breakfast at home. There never is. And if the teacher notices that she's hungry, she has a chance at some food. Angie gets herself dressed in clothes from yesterday—and two days before that. They're the cleanest looking ones.

When she gets to her third-grade classroom, she's subjected to the gibes and teasing of her classmates. That's the only time they even talk to her because Angie sometimes smells from not having a bath and wearing dirty clothes.

She also gets teased because she's a slow reader and has other trouble in the classroom. Sometimes she gets very mad and gets in trouble with the teacher. Even though things don't usually go well at school, Angie hangs around until the end of the day because she doesn't want to go home. There are no friends. No real toys to play with—unless you call meth tools toys.

She knows her mother will be "cooking," but it won't be dinner. Also, Mom's and Dad's "friends" are always dropping by, and some of them are too friendly with Angie. Sometimes they touch her inappropriately. But it's Angie who gets in trouble. Then, her parents beat her. When the day is finally over, Angie tries to fall asleep to the constant noises of cooking, and all of the yelling. Her parents and their friends are always yelling.

It is crucial that law enforcement work closely with Child Protective Services and others to give children like Angie the help and support they need to have happy, healthy, and fulfilling childhoods.

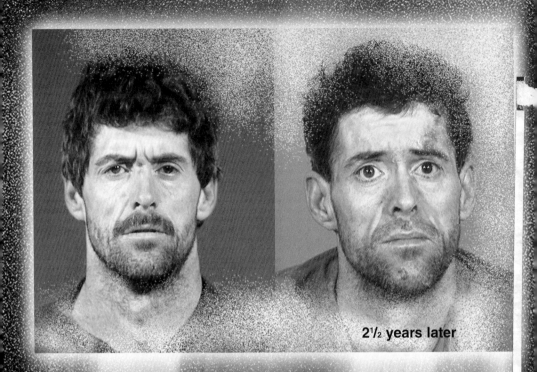
2¹/₂ years later

Chapter 5

Methamphetamine —The Cost to Society

Many people believe that if they don't use methamphetamine, the drug will not affect them. However, with a methamphetamine epidemic sweeping the nation, that's not the case. This is especially true due to the spread of small home-based methamphetamine labs throughout the country.

The Impact of High Hospital Costs Most methamphetamine makers are unemployed and uninsured. Many are on Medicaid—a government insurance program for people who can't afford insurance. However, Medicaid does not pay hospitals and burn centers nearly as much as it costs them to treat these meth victims.

The cost of treating a patient with burns can be quite high. Depending on the nature of the injury and the extent of the care needed, a day at a burn center may cost as much as $10,000. Yet hospitals usually recover only about 30 percent of their costs from state Medicaid plans. In one case, the hospital bill for a methamphetamine-lab burn victim came to $553,000, but Medicaid paid only $110,000. In some areas, burn centers lose between $5 million and $10 million a year for unpaid care. Therefore, as the number of methamphetamine-lab patients rises, these medical centers are forced to operate at greater-than-ever losses.

In some instances, the end result may prove disastrous. As Dr. Jeffrey Guy, of the Vanderbilt University Burn Center, put it, "If we continue to take on this large burden, I don't know if we will have a burn unit five or 10 years from now." Vanderbilt is certainly not the only burn center/hospital feeling the pinch. In numerous institutions, as many as one-third of the patients are meth-lab burn victims on Medicaid. This just adds to the pressure in an already overburdened health-care system.

Crime, Fear, and Costs

Methamphetamine labs take a serious toll on society in other ways as well. When a methamphetamine lab moves into a community, it usually isn't too long before a substantial amount of crime, fear, and economic loss follows. Just having an illegal drug making operation in the neighborhood frequently brings in criminals and leads to an array of crimes that range from identity theft to homicide.

Police reports show a distinct connection between the incidence of violent crime and the degree of methamphetamine use in a community. In many areas, plans to build

This neighborhood is watching

The Partnership for a Drug-Free America®

END METH
Go to drugfree.org/ENDMETH

As public education on how to spot meth labs continues, many neighborhoods are indeed watching for the telltale signs of drug production.

larger jail facilities are under way, since people arrested for methamphetamine crimes are causing these buildings to overflow. In Knox County, Indiana, methamphetamine-related cases once made up about 20 percent of the court's caseload, but in recent years, the number of cases has skyrocketed. Now, in about 75 percent of the cases that reach court, the use or manufacture of methamphetamine is a factor. Methamphetamine has also driven up violent crime in the Southwest. This was evident in the murder of three people in Hogback, New Mexico. According to federal authorities, the execution-style murders resulted from a methamphetamine deal that had gone bad.

As methamphetamine use spreads, the violence associated with it can touch anyone at anytime. In Nevada County,

California, it took its toll on a well-liked yoga instructor and mother of two, who was abducted in broad daylight after leaving an ATM machine.

Her assailant was twenty-three-year-old Jacob Hill, who is currently serving thirty-four years to life for the crime. His victim reported that after looking into Hill's eyes, she could see that he was high on something. That "something" turned out to be methamphetamine coupled with another "speed up" drug that Hill had taken before going out that day.

Hill had been addicted to methamphetamine for about ten years when he kidnapped and assaulted the yoga instructor. His introduction to the drug came in his first year of high school, when he was just thirteen. A friend whose father had been manufacturing methamphetamine at home had offered him some. His friend hardly fit the stereotype of a drug user; he was a popular boy who was on the football team.

Nevertheless, the drug proved to be the undoing of Jacob Hill. He soon became addicted to it and before long methamphetamine dominated his life. He developed a hundred-dollar-a-day habit and did not graduate from high school. Instead, he became involved in crime to get the money he needed to buy the methamphetamine he craved. Following a stint in prison, Hill was finally off the drug and managed to stay that way for a time. He married and was delighted to learn that his wife was expecting a baby boy.

However, the joy was short-lived. Hill turned to methamphetamine again after learning that he had an incurable eye disease that would eventually cause him to lose his vision. One day, while on the drug, he flew into a methamphetamine-related tirade and hurt his wife. He was subsequently convicted on spouse abuse charges and sent to a treatment center for drug addiction.

While at the center, Hill said that he met a doctor who was also being treated for a drug problem at the facility. According to Hill, the doctor gave him a prescription for Adderall—an amphetamine that would intensify the effects of methamphetamine. Supposedly, on the day of the kidnapping, Hill had taken a double dose of Adderall along with methamphetamine.

As with many meth-related violent crimes, the result had

CAR CRASHES AND METHAMPHETAMINE

Methamphetamine use has had deadly consequences on the road. This was especially evident in a courtroom in West Valley City, Utah, in March 2004. There, a nineteen-year-old was sentenced for up to thirty years in prison for automobile homicide. While high on methamphetamine, the teen had run over three young siblings. Two of the children died, while the third survived but was left crippled by the accident. On the day of the driver's sentencing, the six-year-old survivor came into court with his legs supported by metal braces. He wanted to ask the convicted driver why he ran over and killed his brother and sister.

There have been numerous other fatal road accidents caused by drivers high on methamphetamine. In February 2004, a California truck driver on methamphetamine crashed his vehicle, killing two other drivers on the road that day. The truck driver had been traveling at a speed of more than 90 miles (145 km) an hour. He said that he'd had to speed to escape the gang of "gargoyles" that were chasing him.

tragic consequences for both Hill and his victim. The woman he kidnapped endured a horrendous experience, while Jacob Hill is likely to spend nearly the rest of his life in prison.

The High Cost of Methamphetamine

Law-enforcement personnel have had to handle other similarly horrific methamphetamine-related crimes. At times, individuals within the methamphetamine trade have dealt violently with each other, and their actions have taken a toll on community resources as well. That was the case with George, a former methamphetamine dealer, who wanted to leave the drug world for good. In January 2000, he arranged to settle a debt with his business partner that he hoped would allow him to finally start on a new path. However, leaving the business turned out to be more difficult than he thought. His partner had other ideas about both the amount George owed and his freedom to walk away from their undertakings. Some men his partner hired forcibly took George to an isolated cabin. There, they poured gasoline over him and lit a match.

George later woke up in a hospital room with third- and fourth-degree burns over a good part of his body. He was in terrible pain. "Being burned is the worst experience

METHAMPHETAMINE AND CAR THEFT

At times law-enforcement authorities have dealt with waves of methamphetamine-related car theft. In these cases, the methamphetamine cooks usually sell some of the cars for cash. They turn the rest into mobile methamphetamine labs.

According to Utah's Department of Public Safety, a single methamphetamine-lab fire in an apartment building there caused extensive
damage. Twelve units of the apartments at the site were completely
destroyed, while another twelve were badly damaged. The total
damage was estimated at $1,650,000 and displaced forty people.
The meth-lab operator later died as well.

anyone can suffer," he said. "I wouldn't wish it on my
worst enemy. I don't wish it on the people who did this."

Nonviolent Crime

Even methamphetamine-related
crime that isn't violent can be costly to society. Police have
found that a high number of identity-theft cases are tied to
methamphetamine use. These thieves have become quite
expert at robbing mailboxes. They forge and alter checks as
well as send in preapproved credit-card applications. When
the credit cards arrive, they use the money to buy chemicals
to make more methamphetamine as well as for other items.
During a methamphetamine-lab raid in Westminster,
Colorado, the North Metro Drug Task Force found a large
garbage bag filled with mail. They later learned that more
than twenty people were involved in mail and identity theft to
support an ongoing methamphetamine manufacturing operation. Such thefts result in a loss of both time and money for
the people and businesses that fall victim to them.

For retailers selling cold remedies containing ingredients used to make methamphetamine theft can be a
serious problem as well. Some stores report losses as high
as 25 percent on such products due to theft. Farmers,

In 2005 Oregon became the first state to require prescriptions for certain cold medicines that contain ingredients used to make meth. Oregon law now requires customers to provide photo ID and sign a logbook every time they purchase these cold medicines.

along with agricultural suppliers, are also targeted by methamphetamine makers. Some fertilizers that farmers frequently purchase in large quantities are another ingredient used to make methamphetamine.

Environmental Pollution

Methamphetamine is further costly to society as meth labs pollute the environment and depress property values in the areas where they are located. When a methamphetamine lab is discovered, the property owner is responsible for cleaning up the house, apartment, motel, shed, or other location. The cleanup and decontamination required by law is intensive and extremely costly. The price of a methamphetamine lab cleanup can range from $3,000 to $150,000. As noted by the Safe Streets Campaign in Tacoma, Washington, the existence of a single meth lab can negatively affect a significant number of people:

> When a meth lab is next door, it not only negatively impacts the property value of that home, but the surrounding homes as well. Even after people succeed in getting neighborhood meth labs closed down, the costs continue to mount up. . . . When owners can't afford to clean up the property, or when court proceedings leave these houses in legal limbo, they may be boarded up and left vacant for months or years. Even after a former meth lab property is restored, it can take years to reverse the negative impact on the value of houses in the neighborhood.

Still Other Costs

Methamphetamine is costly to society in still other ways as well. Special training for firefighters and police has been needed to deal with the hazards meth labs present. Expensive protective gear and new decontamination equipment have strained the budgets of these service units in many areas. The drug has also stretched the nation's already overburdened legal

Because the chemical fumes are so deadly, the cleanup of a meth lab is now handled by heavily protected haz-mat (hazardous materials) teams—at least in those places that can afford the huge expense.

system, as cases involving methamphetamine fill the courts and convicted meth cooks and dealers are sent to prison. To worsen matters, the children of methamphetamine users and methamphetamine cooks have flooded the foster care system. Increasing numbers of these young people have had to be taken from parents who could no longer care for them properly. Undoubtedly, methamphetamine's effects are far reaching. In terms of the economy, the environment, and the fabric of society, the drug takes a serious toll.

3 months later

Chapter 6

THE SPREAD OF METHAMPHETAMINE —CAN IT BE STOPPED?

Can the present methamphetamine epidemic be stopped? That's a complex question to which there is no easy answer. Some people see drug treatment programs as the way to beat the methamphetamine problem. In the last decade or so, there's been a dramatic rise in treatment-center admissions for people addicted to methamphetamine. The number rose from 28,000 admissions in 1993 to 129,079 in 2004. The need for methamphetamine treatment on a national level was sufficiently great to warrant a federal budget of $473.8 million in 2006 to fight methamphetamine abuse on a number of levels.

Since the year 2000, the need for methamphetamine addiction treatment has risen in nearly every state. This frequently occurs when the popularity of a highly addictive drug increases. The Alcohol and Drug Abuse Division of Colorado's Department of Human Services reported that admissions for methamphetamine treatment had risen 253 percent in five years—from 1,314 in 2000 to 4,645 in 2005. In addition, the number of methamphetamine users visiting emergency departments in Denver rose from 63 in 2003 to 986 in 2005. These figures reflect a national trend.

Treatment

Yet treating methamphetamine addicts has never been easy. Often, drug counselors report that these are their most difficult clients. This is largely due to the highly addictive nature of the drug and the chemical changes in the brain that result from its use. While in treatment, people addicted to methamphetamine are encouraged to develop a plan for a lifelong recovery. They need to change the way they think and act when it comes to the drug. This is known as a cognitive-behavioral therapy approach. They have to be able to identify triggers or situations that could lead them to begin using the drug again and be prepared to fight their cravings.

An especially difficult time for recovering methamphetamine addicts frequently occurs about 45 to 120 days into their treatment. At this point, they hit a period in which their bodies experience physiological changes that include intense cravings for the drug. This has wrongly led some people to believe that methamphetamine addicts are untreatable.

Though research indicates that methamphetamine addicts generally need longer and more intensive treatment than do people addicted to other drugs, these individuals often do well in highly structured programs where they work closely with their counselors. It's vital that people battling a methamphetamine addiction learn to avoid risky activities such as

DRUG-FREE SCHOOLS FOR RECOVERING TEEN ADDICTS

Some states have established special high schools for students recovering from methamphetamine and other drug addictions. These facilities are much like other high schools—they offer the same types of courses and after-school activities and clubs. The big difference, however, is that abstinence from drugs is the norm here and everyone is striving to stay drug-free.

Almost all the students at these schools still see their drug counselors on a regular basis. They also receive credit for attending weekly sessions in which they discuss their feelings about staying drug-free and the challenges they face daily. At most of these schools, a student who slips will be given another chance if he or she admits what happened and continues to work at staying clean and sober. Those who don't are asked to leave the school.

These alternative schools are extremely popular, and often there's a waiting list to get in. As Judy Hanson, the director of Sobriety High in Minnesota, put it, "[The students] learn that it isn't going to be boring to be sober, which is what they're fearing. But we've got a wide range of very interesting students. We've got athletes. We've got musicians. These kids are fun. This isn't a boring place."

drinking alcohol or visiting old friends and hangouts where methamphetamine is still part of the scene. To truly recover, they have to change their entire lifestyle.

The newest research shows that brain scans of recovering methamphetamine addicts are often strikingly similar to those of patients suffering from depression and anxiety. This has led researchers to believe that medicating recovering methamphetamine addicts for these conditions could significantly aid in the recovery process. As senior research scientist Edythe London, Ph.D., noted, "Treating methamphetamine addicts typically focuses on addressing drug craving. These PET images [brain scans] pinpoint, for the first time, abnormal [brain] activity that is closely linked to symptoms of depression and anxiety. Targeting these complicating conditions as part of a more comprehensive treatment program may improve success rates for methamphetamine addiction therapy."

Doing More While treatment for those addicted to methamphetamine is crucial, many people believe that the methamphetamine problem needs to be tackled on a broader level. Unless the availability of methamphetamine is curtailed, there will never be enough treatment centers to deal with all the drug's victims. The toll in human suffering for men, women, and children in much of the United States will also rise immeasurably.

When trying to ban illegal substances, government agencies generally go after the big-time suppliers and dealers. However, in dealing with methamphetamine, this strategy needs to be altered, since small-time meth cooks with fairly small meth labs largely characterize this drug landscape. Here, lawmakers have had to resort to different tactics. One has been to cut off meth cooks from the supplies they need.

Cutting Off Supplies As all methamphetamine

recipes rely on certain key ingredients, states began passing laws to limit access to over-the-counter medications containing the highly desired substances. In 2004 Oklahoma passed the first law—and one of the strictest—requiring that all such medications be kept behind the pharmacy counter or in a locked case. Customers wishing to purchase these drugs are required to produce a photo ID as well as sign a special register or receipt for these items. The law limits the quantity of these drugs that a person can purchase in a one-month period as well.

The Oklahoma legislation impedes methamphetamine production in other ways, too. People possessing large amounts of other ingredients commonly used to make methamphetamine can be charged with *intent* to manufacture the drug. Plus, under the Oklahoma law, judges can deny bail to individuals charged with cooking up batches of methamphetamine. Oklahoma is certainly not the only state that's turned to legislation to fight methamphetamine—about forty other states have enacted similar laws.

A number of new state laws have also tried to limit access to certain crop fertilizers frequently used to manufacture methamphetamine. In some states, free locks have been distributed to farmers to safeguard their tanks from break-ins. A number of the chemical fertilizer companies are taking steps to limit potential theft as well. Author Dirk Johnson described one such solution in his book, *Meth: The Home-Cooked Menace*:

One company is marketing a solution that dyes the colorless gas a pinkish hue. If thieves steal the fertilizer, the dye leaves [pink] stains on their skin and clothes, as well as on the ground around their tanks. The color signals to farmers that intruders have disturbed their tanks. It also helps law enforcement authorities track down the pink-stained meth cooks. Even the meth made from [the fertilizer] will have the stain.

Other companies are working on changing the formula used to manufacture certain fertilizers. They hope to allow them to retain their effectiveness as a fertilizer while rendering them useless to meth cooks.

Action on a National Level State laws as well as efforts to alter typical methamphetamine ingredients have been helpful. However, a giant step forward in the fight against methamphetamine came on March 2, 2006, when Congress passed the first-ever comprehensive methamphetamine legislation. Known as the Combat Methamphetamine Epidemic Act, this legislation was attached to the new provisions of the Patriot Act. Representative Chris Cannon of Utah noted that in passing the bill, Congress struck a blow against a different kind of terrorist—the kind that produces and sells this dangerous drug.

The Combat Methamphetamine Epidemic Act is the first broad-scale anti-meth legislation designed to uniformly fight methamphetamine use throughout the nation. Previous legislation proposed by individual members of Congress provided stand-alone solutions to single aspects of the meth problem. However, this legislation took a broader approach by targeting every angle of methamphetamine trafficking—

ingredient supply control, environmental regulation, and criminal prosecution. Modeled after the successful Oklahoma law, the new federal legislation contains the following provisions, among others:

- Prohibits individuals from purchasing more than a certain amount of key cold medicines in a day or in thirty days
- Requires that these medicines be sold from behind the counter or kept in a locked cabinet
- Requires that individuals show ID and sign a logbook upon purchasing the medicines
- Imposes quantity restrictions and reporting requirements on mail order, Internet, and flea-market sales of the medicines
- Toughens federal penalties for methamphetamine traffickers and smugglers as well as those who cook or deal methamphetamine in the presence of children
- Requires reporting from major cold medicine importers and exporters and holds them responsible for their efforts to prevent their products from being misused

The new law largely resulted from the work of the Congressional Caucus to Fight and Control Methamphetamine. The group, made up of 140 members of Congress, works to raise national awareness of the dangers posed by methamphetamine abuse and to advance strong public policy to fight against meth manufacturing, distribution, and use. The caucus involves state and community leaders, law-enforcement officials, public health officers, and advocacy groups in developing the means to address this complex problem.

In December 2005, Senate Majority Leader Bill Frist, Senator James Talent, Senator Dianne Feinstein and various law-enforcement leaders held a press conference to lend bipartisan support to the inclusion of anti-methamphetamine provisions in the Patriot Act legislation.

The strategy behind the new anti-methamphetamine law designed by the caucus is clear. It's ultimately more effective to limit the available ingredient supply than to try to apprehend every user and small-time meth cook. As one undercover narcotics officer put it, "It's absurd to think we're going to make even a dent in meth by busting [methamphetamine users and cooks]. There's way too many of them. And it takes too long to bust them." These sentiments were echoed by Nancy Pellow, an analyst with the Oklahoma state legislature, who noted, "It didn't matter if we took [methamphetamine

Using the Law to Stop Meth Cooks

Different states have tried different ways to stop methamphetamine production in their areas. Illinois passed a law establishing a meth-manufacturer registry similar to the state sex-offender registries. The names of individuals convicted of manufacturing methamphetamine are posted online. Other detailed information is supplied as well, such as the person's birth date, conviction date, and where the crime occurred.

users and cooks] off the street and put them in jail. Chances are they'd be out soon and go back to making meth. And when you took one away, ten more would step in to take their place."

Involving the Community The Meth Watch program has also taken root in many parts of the country. Through this endeavor, clerks in retail stores are trained to be alert to the signs of customer theft related to making meth-amphetamine. An example of Meth Watch at its best occurred at a Kmart in a small midwestern town. There, one of the store clerks single-handedly foiled a meth cook's operation.

It happened when a customer at the store decided to buy most of his methamphetamine supplies at Kmart that day. First, he picked up a substantial quantity of propane along with a number of other items he'd need to brew the drug. Then he wheeled his shopping cart over to the store's pharmacy and purchased the cold and allergy pills he'd need. After that, the customer headed straight for the store's men's room.

The clerk, who'd noticed the man's unusual assortment of purchases, also noticed that this customer was spending an especially long time in the men's room. The clerk went to check on the situation and found that the man had set up a makeshift methamphetamine lab in a men's-room stall! The police were called and the man was arrested on the spot. In some areas, Meth Watch also trains community members to be alert to the visible signs of operating meth labs. These volunteers notify authorities of any suspicious activities so such situations can be speedily checked out.

Still another way to fight the methamphetamine epidemic has been through the creation of drug courts across the country. A drug court is a specialized court that combines the resources of a judge, a prosecutor from the district attorney's office, social workers, chemical dependency counselors, mental health workers, and others in rehabilitating drug offenders. The drug court endeavors to keep the individual off methamphetamine or other drugs through intensive intervention designed to significantly change that person's lifestyle.

A methamphetamine abuser could ideally choose the drug court intervention over doing time in a traditional prison setting. The drug court program offers the addicted person an individualized treatment plan designed to meet that person's unique needs. Nevertheless, in most cases, the drug abuser will still have to attend a highly structured regimen of classes, as well as counseling sessions several times a week. In addition, regular attendance at Narcotics Anonymous and Alcoholics Anonymous meetings may be required. People in drug court programs generally have to meet all the program requirements for at least a year. Some participants feel that while in the program they become so focused on recovery that they do not have the time or energy to focus on anything more negative— such as methamphetamine.

A key consideration that's an important plus in these programs is that the addicted individual only has to meet the requirements of a single plan. In the past, drug abusers often had to meet varying requirements set by probation officers, the court, a mental health center, and in some cases, child welfare services. It would be difficult for almost anyone to meet the stringent requirements of all these agencies, but it has often been nearly impossible for methamphetamine abusers struggling to get their lives back on track to do so.

In the early stages of the drug court process, the drug abuser sees the judge about once a week. Prior to that meeting, the judge meets with and reviews reports from the person's social worker and mental health counselor as well and has looked over the individual's drug test results. One judge described her role as being that of a judge, preacher, and social worker rolled into one.

This consistent and continual contact would be lacking if a methamphetamine addict were forced to deal with his or her problems through criminal court. In that situation, things like hearings, pleadings, and extensions usually come up at six-month intervals. Under those circumstances, it's difficult for a judge to remember the details of all the cases he or she is assigned. Yet in drug court, the judge is frequently in contact with the drug offenders, and therefore remains aware of the various aspects of the different assigned cases.

Those who favor drug courts see them as a more enlightened way to deal with methamphetamine abusers. It offers them a real chance for rehabilitation rather than the usual revolving door in and out of prison. However, drug courts work only if the judge has a solid support system to refer drug abusers to. Without adequate mental health and social services, the program won't work, and unfortunately in some rural areas such services are not always readily available.

However, where adequate backup services are on hand, drug courts appear to go a long way in doing the job. To some, these courts may seem like an expensive alternative, but in the long run they are not. Such treatment programs cost from about $6,000 to $8,000 a year, while the cost of keeping someone in prison for a year is about $20,000. Few places can afford to build sufficient prisons for all the people with drug-related offenses. Therefore, in many cases, drug courts fill an important need.

Mexican Drug-Cartels However, regardless of the services available to drug abusers, the methamphetamine problem in the United States may prove to be even more difficult to curtail than initially thought. As the numbers of small methamphetamine labs are reduced, the larger, well-organized professional drug rings have once again moved onto the meth scene. For example, in Oklahoma, the number of small methamphetamine lab seizures fell 90 percent since its 2004 anti-methamphetamine law went into effect. Yet at the same time, seizures of the drug from Mexican cartels increased nearly fivefold.

These Mexican drug cartels have come up with an even stronger form of methamphetamine, known as ice. As one drug-enforcement agent described it, "Ice is to meth, what crack is to cocaine." Since crack is a more potent, highly addictive form of cocaine, this does not bode well for the meth scene. The ice produced at the Mexican cartel superlabs is known to be both extremely powerful and pure.

In drug busts made at some of these Mexican cartel superlabs, law-enforcement authorities have found evidence of a potentially huge operation. At times, they've uncovered

ACCIDENTAL OVERDOSE

The increased purity in the methamphetamine purchased from the Mexican drug cartels has led to a rise in methamphetamine overdoses. Many methamphetamine addicts don't realize that the new drug is going to be so much stronger than what they are used to. A user may usually take one-fourth of a gram, but now that same amount has doubled or tripled in potency. In some areas, the difference in strength has resulted in an increased number of emergency-room visits and even deaths.

hundreds of thousands of cold pills that have been smuggled in from overseas and Canada. These labs often receive monthly supplies of massive quantities of tablets from rogue chemical companies that frequently have little to do with the legitimate retail drug businesses or health-care industries.

According to the National Drug Intelligence Center, the largest Mexican organizations have production operations in both Mexico and the United States. In some cases, lab sites capable of producing more than 200 pounds (91 kg) of methamphetamine have been found in the United States.

In a Mexican cartel superlab, manufacturing the drug depends on people performing four specific roles. The lab manager oversees the entire operation and is usually a highly trusted leader or member of the organization. The person second in charge is the meth cook. These cooks are also well trusted and tend to be quite experienced at producing quality methamphetamine. The cook instructs and supervises the lab workers but personally performs tasks that require more skill, such as mixing and heating the chemicals.

The lab workers are the least valued individuals at the site. They carry out the most hazardous tasks as well as those that require physical labor. The cartels also post a security staff at every lab. These guards protect the lab from other criminal organizations as well as law enforcement. They also keep an eye on the lab workers and stop any of them who may wish to leave before the cooking process is completed.

The individuals running these operations are not addicts who are high on the drug, but shrewd businesspeople anxious to tap into a ready and waiting market. As a Drug Enforcement Administration notice described them: "Mexican organizations first infiltrate the market by offering high quality methamphetamine at low prices, amassing a large customer base that comes to prefer the superior product over the locally produced 'hillbilly meth.' Once the customer base is firmly established, they raise prices."

The notice further states that such operations are "currently under way" across America's landscape. The rise in methamphetamine prices has already led to a spike in crime in some areas. Burglaries have been shown to be on the rise in areas where meth use is especially heavy. This may be partly because

TRANSPORTATION

The Mexican drug cartels like to use cars to transport the chemicals needed to make methamphetamine as well as the finished product. Often, these vehicles have been outfitted with special hidden compartments in which to keep the chemicals or methamphetamine while on the road. Both tractor-trailer rigs and small aircraft are also used to transport methamphetamine, especially large loads. To send small amounts of the drug to individual customers, Mexican drug cartels have even used the U.S. Postal Service at times. This has allowed them to further expand their distribution markets.

users now need even more cash to support their drug habit.

Some people believe strongly that the problem ultimately rests with the fact that while any number of laws can be passed and enforced, it's impossible to legislate away demand for a drug. As long as people want methamphetamine and are willing to pay for it, it is highly likely that there will be someone willing to take the risks to provide it.

Stopping the Epidemic

Unfortunately, the demand for methamphetamine remains great. In 2006 the UN's *World Drug Report* cited methamphetamine as the most abused drug on earth with 26,000,000 meth addicts throughout the world. There are 1,400,000 methamphetamine users in the United States alone, and the number is rising. Clearly, drug-enforcement authorities have their work cut out for them in the fight against this drug.

Yet they hope to be well armed in this important battle, as government agencies are relying on still another weapon in the fight against methamphetamine. These are the strategic partnerships forged with private-sector groups to launch public-awareness campaigns. Many of these are directed at teens and center on the negative consequences of making bad decisions regarding methamphetamine use.

In June 2006, the Partnership for a Drug-Free America, along with the White House Office of National Drug Control Policy, introduced a new media campaign aimed at preventing methamphetamine use in Latino communities across the United States. The English/Spanish-language campaign messages, which include public service advertisements for television, radio, and print, are the largest-scale Spanish-language anti-meth effort to date.

If roaches can survive a nuclear holocaust, why won't they go near a meth lab?

[Think about it.]

META

Your future stops here.™

Aimed at the meth manufacturer as well as the user, this methprevention.com poster cites the fact that even the cockroach, the ultimate evolutionary survivor, won't hang out in a meth lab.

The campaign was created following a new study by Partnership for a Drug-Free America indicating that Latino youths were nearly twice as likely to have tried methamphetamine than were white or African American young people.

Rats love
human waste,
but can't stand
to be near
a meth lab.

[Think about it.]

⚠ META

Your future stops here.™

A poster informing people that a rat prefers conditions in a field of human waste to those in a meth lab is intended to make one think twice before starting — or even setting foot in — a meth lab.

This came as a shock to many, since historically, illegal drug use in Latino communities has been lower than in either white or African American communities. However, the study data indicated an unsettling departure from that trend. In the study, Latino meth use was on a par with that of whites and was far higher than that of African American or Asian populations.

In response, a series of graphic media messages, available in both Spanish and English, were created to paint a revealing portrait of the devastating physical and psychological consequences of methamphetamine use. One television spot, entitled "Head," features a young girl talking to her friend, who plays down the dangers of methamphetamine use. As the young meth user speaks, her sunglasses are removed to reveal sunken eyes. Next, a scarf is taken off to show the telltale skin lesions common among meth users.

ONE TIME.
YOU'RE HOOKED.
METH. YOUR FUTURE STOPS HERE.™

www.methprevention.com

Methprevention.com offers a literal interpretation of "getting hooked." The message that one-time use means addiction rather than leads to addiction is erroneous, but the image is nonetheless a powerful reminder of what could be in store for a teen who chooses to take meth.

Last, when the young meth user smiles, she shows off a mouthful of loose, rotting teeth. It's a frightening but revealing commentary, and a number of similar television and print ads have been created as well.

Will the combined effect of more encompassing laws, better enforcement policies, and mass media campaigns be enough to win the fight against methamphetamine? Some believe that these efforts will surely make a significant dent in the widespread use of this very destructive drug. Others think that the problem is too far out of control and that methamphetamine will remain high on the list of popular drugs until the next trendy drug comes along. Who is right? Only time will tell.

GLOSSARY

addiction: a disease characterized by compulsive drug seeking as well as by changes in the brain resulting from drug use

chronic: a continuing or ongoing disease

convulsions: violent muscular contractions or spasms of the body

crashing: an unpleasant sensation following a methamphetamine high, characterized by feelings of anxiety, depression, and irritability

craving: a powerful, often uncontrollable desire for drugs

dopamine: an important pleasure-related brain chemical

euphoria: a heightened sense of well-being or joy

hallucinate: to see or hear something that is not there

hyperthermia: raised body temperature

invulnerability: a feeling of having no weaknesses or of not being able to be hurt

meth mouth: a condition in which an ongoing methamphetamine user loses teeth as a result of meth-related tooth decay and gum disease

paranoid: a mental state in which an individual is overly suspicious of others without cause

pharmacological: the science of the nature and action of drugs

rush: an intensely pleasurable feeling experienced after smoking or intravenously injecting methamphetamine, which is also known as a flush

serotonin: an important pleasure-related brain chemical

stamina: strength or endurance

stimulant: a drug that increases or intensifies the rate of the body's vital functions

toxic: drug effects that are poisonous and detrimental to the functioning of an organ or a group of organs

tremors: a shaking movement

withdrawal: a variety of physical and emotional symptoms that occur after use of an addictive drug is stopped or reduced

Source Notes

8   Dirk Johnson, *Meth: The Home-Cooked Menace* (Center City, MN: Hazelden Foundation, 2005), 87.

9   Ibid.

9   National Institute on Drug Abuse, *Community Drug Bulletin Alert* (Rockville, MD: U.S. Department of Health and Human Services, October, 1998), unpaged.

10   Center for Substance Abuse Prevention, *Meth: What's Cooking In Your Neighborhood?* (DHHS Publication No. SMA 3710A; U.S. Department of Health and Human Services, 2002), 6.

14   Dirk Johnson, 8.

16   National Institute on Drug Abuse, *Monitoring the Future, National Results on Adolescent Drug Use, Overview of Key Findings, 2005*. Bethseda, MD: U.S. Department of Health and Human Services, 2005, p.24.

17   David J. Jefferson, "America's Most Dangerous Drug," *Newsweek*, August 8, 2005, 40.

17   Dominic Ippolito, "My Life as a Drug Dealer," MSNBC-Newsweek Society, August 1, 2005 http://www.msnbc.msn.com/id/8790494/site/newsweek/ (accessed July 12, 2006).

18   Jessica L. Sandham, "Cranked Up," *Education Week*, May 24, 2000, 36.

18   "Crime Soaring as Meth Snags Young Users," *The Arizona Republic*, April 24, 2006 www.azcentral.com (accessed May 3, 2006).

18   Ibid.

19   Ibid.

19   Ibid.

21   Dirk Johnson, 89.

23   Ibid, 90.

23   Samantha Johnson, "Culture of Meth: Poor Man's Cocaine Often Creeps Up on Those Who Use It," *Craig Daily Press*, May 11, 2004, 1.

25   Center for Substance Abuse Protection, *Meth: What's Cooking In Your Neighborhood?*, 3.

26   Barbara Hastings, "The Users: Their Stories; Paranoia, Voices, Crawling Bugs," *Star-Bulletin & Advertiser*, February 5, 1989, A1.

26   Kimberly Mills, "The Dangers of Meth Cannot Be Understated," *Seattle Post-Intelligencer*, December 13, 1999, A11.

29   Ibid.

29   Center for Substance Abuse Protection, *Meth: What's Cooking in Your Neighborhood?* 5.

30   Mills, A11.

30   Ibid.

31   Amy Hamilton, "Meth Use Growing Among Teens," *The Craig Daily Press*, May 18, 2004, 11.

33   Mills, A11.

33   Ibid.

34   Northwest HIDTA in cooperation with the Washington State Office of Lieutenant Governor Brad Owen, *A Drug Resource Guide: Quick Facts on Methamphetamine, Ecstasy, GHB & Marijuana* (Winter 2003), 7.

35   Mills, A11.

35   Ibid.

37   Christine Hollister, "One Year Later . . . A Mother Remembers," *Gretna Breeze*, January 12, 2006, A1.

38   Ibid.

42   Catherine Monahan, "Autopsy Showed Drugs Played Part in Hornickel's Death," The Creightonian Online (volume 84, issue 13), January 28, 2005 http://press.creighton.edu/012805/news2.htmef (accessed May 20, 2006).

42   Ibid.

43   Jeffrey Robb, "Hopes Dim for Omaha Woman," *Omaha World-Herald*, January 8, 2005, A01.

43   Joe Dejka, "Finding a Body Doesn't End the Mystery," *Omaha World-Herald*, January 13, 2005, B01.

44   Dirk Johnson, 40.

45   Ibid., 41.

45   Ibid., 58.

47   Ibid., 52.

48   Barbara Marsh, "Meth At Work: In Virtually Every Industry, Use Among Employees Is on the Rise," *Los Angeles Times*, July 7, 1996, A1.

48   Ibid.

48   Ibid.

49   Ibid.

49   Ibid.

50   Marsh, A1.

51 Center for Substance Abuse Prevention, *Tips for Teens: The Truth about Methamphetamine*, 2001. SAMHSA's National Clearing House for Alcohol and Drug Information, Rockville, MD 20847-2345 (1-800-729-6686)

54 Arian Campo-Flores, "The Fallout: 'I Felt My Face Just Melting,'" *Newsweek*, August 8, 2005, 44.

54 Ibid.

55 Sarah Huntley, "Meth's Legacy: Burns, Ruined Lives," *Rocky Mountain News*, March 16, 2002, B1.

55 Ibid.

56 Ibid.

56 Campo-Flores, 44.

57 All quotes for this sidebar were taken from a U.S. Department of the Interior press release entitled, "Coalition Announces $300,000 for Public Awareness Campaign", November 30, 2006.

61 Dennis Wichern, "The War on Meth: A Special Agent Describes Nearly 20 Years of Life on the Front Lines in a Battle Against a Corrosive Drug," MSNBC-Newsweek Society, July 31, 2005 http://www.msnbc.msn.com/id/8760265/site/newsweek/f (accessed May 2, 2006).

66 Karen Swetlow, "Children at Clandestine Methamphetamine Labs: Helping Meth's Youngest Victims," *OVC Bulletin*, June 2003, 3.

67 Brittany Bowman, "The Tightest Grip," Partnership for a Drug-Free America, June 2, 2006 http://www.drugfree.org/Portal/Stories/The_Tightest_Grip (accessed June 12, 2006).

68–69 Prepared Remarks of U.S. Attorney General Alberto Gonzales at the National District Attorneys Association Meeting, Portland, Maine, July 18, 2005, #06212005: Prepared Remarks of Attorney General Albert Gonzales Sentencing Guidelines Speech, http://www.usdoj.gov/ag/speeches/2005/071805nationaldisattassoc meeting(date (accessed May 6, 2006).

69 Ibid.

69–70 Safe Streets Campaign, *Meth Is a Killer; Help Is a Healer* (booklet). Tacoma, Washington: Washington State Methamphetamine Initiative, 2005, 17.

72–73 Swetlow, 4.

76 Campo-Flores, p.44.

80–81 Huntley, B1.

83 Safe Streets Campaign, *Meth Is a Killer; Help Is a Healer* (booklet), 17.

89   Dirk Johnson, 94.

90   Jim Rosack, "Treatment of Meth Users Should Target Mood-
      Disorder Symptoms," *Psychiatric News*, March 5, 2004, 50.

92   Dirk Johnson, 109.

94   Ibid., 104.

94–95 Ibid., 105.

98   Ibid., 112.

100   Ibid., 113.

Selected Bibliography

Braswell, Sterling R. *American Meth: A History of the Methamphetamine Epidemic in America*. New York: iUniverse, 2006.

Colvin, Rod. *Prescription Drug Addiction*. Omaha, NE: Addicus Books, 2002.

Courtwright, David T. *Forces of Habit: Drugs and the Making of the Modern World*. Cambridge, MA: Harvard University Press, 2002.

Drug and Alcohol Services Information System. *The DASIS Report: Trends in Methamphetamine/Amphetamine Admissions to Treatment: 1993–2003*. Rockville, MD: Office of Applied Studies, Substance Abuse and Mental Health Services Administration, 2006.

Gahlinquer, Paul M. *Illegal Drugs: A Complete Guide to Their History, Chemistry, Use and Abuse*. Salt Lake City, UT: Sagebrush Press, 2001.

Goldstein, Avram. *Addiction: From Biology to Drug Policy*. New York: Oxford University Press, 2001.

Goode, Erich. *Drugs in American Society*. New York: McGraw-Hill Humanities, 2004.

Hatch, Orrin G., ed. *Losing Ground Against Drugs: The Erosion of America's Borders: Congressional Hearings*. Darby, PA: DIANE, 1999.

Iversen, Leslie. *Speed, Ecstasy, Ritalin: The Science of Amphetamines*. New York: Oxford University Press, 2006.

Johnson, Dirk. *Meth: The Home-Cooked Menace*. Center City, MN: Hazelden Foundation, 2005.

Landry, Mim J. *Understanding Drugs of Abuse: The Process of*

Addiction, Treatment, and Recovery. Arlington, VA: American Psychiatric Publishing, 1994.

Orcutt, James D. *Drugs, Alcohol, and Social Problems*. Summit, PA: Rowman and Littlefield, 2003.

Stares, Paul B. *Global Habit: The Drug Problem in a Borderless World*. Washington, DC: Brookings Institute, 1996.

Wilson, Richard, and Cheryl Kolander. *Drug Abuse Prevention: A School and Community Partnership*. Sudbury, MA: Jones and Bartlett, 2002.

Further Reading and Websites

Books

Bayer, Linda N. *Drugs, Crime, and Criminal Justice*. Philadelphia: Chelsea House, 2001.

Hyde, Margaret O. *Drugs 101: An Overview for Teens*. Minneapolis, MN: Twenty-First Century Books, 2003.

Jacobson, Robert. *Illegal Drugs: America's Anguish*. Detroit: Thomson/Gale, 2006.

Marcovitz, Hal. *Methamphetamine*. San Diego, CA: Lucent Books, 2005.

Mehling, Randi. *Hallucinogens*. Philadelphia: Chelsea House, 2003.

Menhard, Francha Rolfe. *The Facts About Amphetamines*. Tarrytown, NY: Marshall Cavendish, 2005.

Mintzer, Richard. *Meth & Speed = Busted!* Berkeley Heights, NJ: Enslow, 2005.

Olive, Foster M. *Designer Drugs*. Philadelphia: Chelsea House, 2004.

Spalding, Frank. *Methamphetamine: The Dangers of Crystal Meth*. New York: Rosen Publishing Group, 2006.

Torr, James D., ed. *Drug Abuse: Opposing Viewpoints*. San Diego, CA: Greenhaven Press, 1999.

Weatherly, Myra. *Ecstasy and Other Designer Drug Dangers*. Berkeley Heights, NJ: Enslow Publishers, 2000.

We6sites

Drug Enforcement Administration – Methamphetamine
http://www.usdoj.gov/dea/concern/meth_factsheet.html
This website provides a good list of fast facts about
methamphetamine.

National Alliance for Drug Endangered Children
http://www.NationalDEC.org
This is the website of an organization concerned with children
endangered by caregivers who manufacture drugs, deal
drugs, or use them.

National Institute on Drug Abuse (NIDA)
http://www.drugabuse.gov
This excellent website offers educational materials along with
relevant facts and figures on illegal drug use in the United
States.

Office of National Drug Control Policy (ONDCP)
http://www.whitehousedrugpolicy.gov
This is a highly informative website on U.S. national drug-
control policy as well as on state and local efforts at drug-
abuse prevention.

StopDrugs.org
http://www.stopdrugs.org/
This website has a good deal of information on drugs—
especially methamphetamine.

Street Drugs

http://www.streetdrugs.org

This is a good informational website containing reports on
drug abuse and related issues.

*U.S. Department of Health and Human Services for Alcohol
and Drug Information (SASMSA Clearinghouse)*

http://www.ncadi.samhsa.gov/

This website is filled with helpful information for individuals
and families struggling with drug addiction.

Ya Ba Fast Facts

http://www.usdoj.gov/ndic/pubs5/5048/index.htm

Visit this website for up-to-date information on Ya Ba—
methamphetamine mixed with caffeine in pill form.

INDEX

PHOTO ACKNOWLEDGMENTS

The images in this book are used with permission of:

© Faces of Meth™. courtesy of Multnomah County Sheriff's Office, Portland, Oregon, pp. 4, 20, 36, 52, 74, 86; U.S. Drug Enforcement Administration, p. 7 (all); © Yoray Liberman/ Getty Images, p. 8; © Brian Kirley/Hulton Archive/Getty Images, p. 13; © Katy Winn/CORBIS, p. 15; AP Photo/James A. Finley, p. 22; © Royalty-Free/CORBIS, p. 24; © Paul Thompson, Kiralee Hayashi, Arthur Toga, Edythe London/ UCLA, p. 28; Courtesy of Robert D. Thomas, DDS, Savannah, TN, p. 32; AP Photo/Sarpy County Sheriff's Office, p. 38; © Bill Greenblatt/CORBIS SYGMA, p. 59; © H. Barrios/ Bakersfield Californian/ZUMA Press, p. 70; © Partnership for a Drug-Free America, p. 77; © Getty Images, pp. 82, 94; © Robert King/ZUMA Press, p. 84; Courtesy of methprevention.com © 2005 MMA Creative, pp. 102, 103, 104.

Front cover: © Mark Allen Johnson/ZUMA Press.

ABOUT THE AUTHOR

Award-winning children's book author Elaine Landau worked as a newspaper reporter, a children's book editor, and a youth services librarian before becoming a full-time writer. She has written more than 300 books for young readers. Among her recent titles are *Smokejumpers, John F. Kennedy Jr.*, and *Suicide Bombers: Foot Soldiers of the Terrorist Movement*, which was named a Notable Social Studies Trade Book for Young People 2007 by the National Council for the Social Studies (NCSS) and the Children's Book Council. Landau has a bachelor's degree in English and Journalism from New York University and a master's degree in Library and Information Science from Pratt Institute. She lives in Miami, Florida, with her husband and son.